BEYOND
THE
Veil

Scott,
the delights in you!

xoxo
Yronne A.

BEYOND
THE
Veil

Answering the Invitation
of the Bridegroom King

Yvonne Allen

BEYOND THE VEIL

Published by Paul & Yvonne Allen | Southlake, Texas

ISBN (Paperback): 979-8-9889023-0-0

ISBN (Hardback): 979-8-9889023-1-7

ISBN (Kindle): 979-8-9889023-2-4

Library of Congress Control Number: 2023914621

Printed in the United States of America

Holy Ghostwriter: Wendy K. Walters | www.wendykwalters.com

Prepared for Publication: www.palmtreeproductions.com

Cover Photo & Author Photo: Abrahanny Rodriguez | www.abrahanny.com

To contact the author:
YVONNEALLEN.COM
info@yvonneallen.com

Dedication

I dedicate this book to my best friends—
Holy Spirit and *Paul Allen.*

Without you, this book would not be possible, and I wouldn't be the woman I am today. Thank you for your continued patience, love, grace, and mercy.

Acknowledgments

I want to express my heartfelt gratitude to the following people who have been instrumental in the creation of this book—

Harriet Enarson

Roshni Distefano

Wendy Walters

Joy Carignan

Lucas Bessey

Dr. Chiqui Wood

Queenie D'Souza

Judah & Alexa Tuvyana

Tamar Albarian

Abrahanny Rodriguez

Jan Greenwood*

Katie Swain*

Mina Duprey*

Kara Miller*

Dr. Teresa Citro*

La'Wana Harris*

Caroline Mahiti*

Philomena D'souza*

Tim Allen*

Stacy Burnett*

Thank you to all those who have also contributed in some way or the other; you are too numerous to mention.

Again, I would like to thank Holy Spirit and Paul Allen—words cannot express my gratitude, and I will forever be indebted to you.

*Beta Group Readers

Let us rejoice and exalt Him and give Him glory, because the wedding celebration of the Lamb has come. **And His bride has made herself ready.** *Fine linen, shining bright and clear, has been given to her to wear, and the fine linen represents the righteous deeds of His holy believers.*

REVELATION 19:7-8, TPT

Praise for Beyond the Veil

Beyond the Veil is the personal journey of Yvonne Allen, from religiously knowing about God to an intimate relationship with Him. Yvonne is a brilliant writer and makes every line jump off the page with meaning and beauty. Her history takes you from life as a Catholic child in Mumbai, steeped in religious tradition, to Canada, then America—where God becomes her constant companion. Her orphan spirit, serving God out of obligation, moves into a life of intimacy and daily communion with her Beloved. Readers travel this journey with her from the confines of her small bedroom in India into the expansive relationship with her Lord that lies *Beyond the Veil*. It is impossible for you to read this book and not accompany Yvonne on the journey of knowing God intimately. I did, and gratefully, will never be the same.

LARRY TITUS
Director of Global Outreach, Kingdom Global Ministries
Colleyville, Texas

I have known Yvonne for almost ten years and witnessed her life's transformation firsthand. This confident, powerful, successful businesswoman speaks of Jesus with sweetness and tenderness. She shares times spent with her "Bridegroom" and how His tenderness has affected her profoundly. This book is an open door. It is an invitation to share in her journey as she has grown in unparalleled life-changing intimacy with God—from insider to outsider, servant to friend, daughter to bride. She writes candidly, extending an invitation that you and I, too, can live in greater intimacy with our loving God, in whose embrace values, attitudes, and actions change for the better.

DR. CHIQUI WOOD

Teacher, Pastor, and Co-Author of The Abba Journey
North Richland Hills, Texas

Beyond the Veil is a testament to the transformative power of the only true and living God that takes readers on a transformative journey of faith, hope, and truth. Through her eloquent prose and heartfelt storytelling, Allen encourages readers to transcend the limitations of the natural world and explore the boundless possibilities of a deeper relationship with Jesus Christ.

Throughout the book, Allen emphasizes the importance of prayer and cultivating a personal relationship with God. She encourages readers to embrace faith as a guiding force, enabling them to navigate life's challenges with resilience and hope. By sharing her experiences and struggles, she creates an authentic and relatable narrative that inspires readers to go deeper in their walk with the Lord.

LA'WANA HARRIS, CIC, CDE, ACC

President and Founder of La'Wana Harris, Inc., and Author of Diversity Beyond
Lip Service: A Coaching Guide for Challenging Bias
Raleigh, North Carolina

Beyond the Veil takes readers on a journey of discovery into the depths of intimacy with Christ. Her story is the American dream of success—until God turned her quest for significance into a pursuit of His presence. This read was truly inspirational and personally challenging to seek after the heart of God.

JOSEPH SAPIENZA

Pastor Emeritus of Celebration International Church
and President of Bread of Compassion
Cooperstown, New York

Reading *Beyond The Veil,* one realizes how God interacts with His faithful children who desire an intimate relationship with their Master, Father, Friend, and Husband. It moved me to desire the same closeness the author experiences with the Lord. The book is written in a warm descriptive manner that makes it easy to read and invites you to become a participant in the miraculous stories that unfold right before your eyes. I am sure it will become one of the best companions to any lover of a good book.

REV. DANIEL ALBARIAN

Lead Pastor, Christian Outreach for Armenians Church
North Hollywood, California

Beyond the Veil is a beautifully described journey of a young woman in search of her true identity in Christ. She burns down each page of her old self, pulling down each fake belief and embracing a new spirit of servanthood to a newer understanding of being in friendship with God and, ultimately, viewing herself as the bride of Christ.

RUBY NAEEM JOHN

Director Member Care Foundation
Islamabad, Pakistan

Behind The Veil is the captivating true story of the life of author Yvonne Allen; coming from a middle-class immigrant family, she managed to adapt to a new country and culture, becoming a wealthy woman while discovering her own identity. It is a beautiful reminder that God is always with us and a delightful invitation to choose to have a deeper relationship with our heavenly Father, our Creator, and our Friend.

PASTORS GUILLERMO AND FLOR PORTAL
Bayside Community Church
Sarasota, Florida

Beyond The Veil is a delightful read full of wisdom and reassurance for those of us who have ever struggled with where we belong in our family, how we identify in this world, and where we belong in our relationship with God. It is sure to take you on a journey from beginning to end!

DR. DEMIRA DEVOIL
Hopeful Arms Foundation
Fort Worth, Texas

What an inspiration and invitation this book is to go deeper with the Father! The first time I heard Yvonne share the details of her relationship and consistency of meeting to develop trust and intimacy with the Holy Spirit, it compelled me to press in deeper. This book will awaken you to the possibilities of what's available to those who value the secret place and desire to go ... *Beyond the Veil.*

AUTUMN DAWSON
ROAR Church Texarkana
Texarkana, Texas

Get ready to go on an incredible journey of discovering identity and intimacy with God. In *Beyond the Veil*, you will be encouraged to know God and find intimate fellowship with Him, in which He will become your everything. You will be built up in your faith. You will also be challenged not to settle for less than that which Father God has for you. Having known Yvonne from her teenage years and seeing what God has done in her life, I can say she has lived and is living out everything she says. I highly recommend this book.

REV. CHAD S. FISHER
Cornerstone Community Church
Alberta, Canada

Working with Yvonne on this project was a pure delight, and we got to know each other intimately during our book interviews. I saw her strength, vulnerability, humor, faith, and the many facets of her beautiful, God-given personality. I immersed myself in her story and got lost in the beautiful expression of her transformation into a confident bride of Christ, exercising all her authority, rights, and privileges with the easy grace of one whose heart is consumed with love and affection and filled with childlike joy. *Beyond the Veil* will captivate your heart.

WENDY K. WALTERS
Ghostwriter, Author, Editor
Corinth, Texas

Contents

PROLOGUE

I dropped off my children at school and headed to the parking lot of Central Market Café in Southlake, Texas. It was 6:55 am, and I watched for the doors to open so I could enter, order a cup of coffee, and make my way to the corner booth I had claimed daily for the past six years.

The server greeted me and asked, "The usual?"

"Yes," I smiled, then headed for my spot. It was an ordinary booth in an ordinary place, but to me, it had become hallowed ground. It was here I met daily with the Trinity—Father, Son, and Holy Spirit. They have become very real to me. Each with a distinct personality and expression, yet uniquely and completely one. I opened my Bible and journal and anxiously awaited whatever they desired to pour into me.

It wasn't always this way. I grew up in India as a good Catholic girl. I followed all the rules, did all the right things, and checked off all the right boxes that would make me acceptable to God and my family. But I did not know Him.

It was not until many years later that I had an encounter with a real and living God who awakened my heart, drew me to His side, and bid me to come and dine. Before then, I was an outsider. I didn't really understand what that meant at the time, but as He drew me into His care, I began to know a sense of belonging like nothing I had ever experienced before.

It did not happen instantly; the progression was not without advances and retreats, but gently and tenderly. They showed me what life in the Kingdom looks like. The further in I went, the further I wanted to go.

It is because of this incredible relationship with God that I write this book. I wish I had known earlier what it was like to be a new creation in Christ. I wish someone had explained how the process of being sanctified and transformed into His image was a journey of falling in love and abiding with Them. My connection with my Father is now so deep and extraordinary; I pray my words will provoke you to jealousy until you burn with the unquenchable desire to know Him more.

In these pages, I share glimpses of my life before, during, and after my transformation. This is not an attempt at a scholarly study or doctoral presentation—it is real, raw, and wrapped in the love of God. I pray as you read my story, it will quicken memories and emotions in you and stir your soul.

Nothing in creation strives to be beautiful. It just is. At the hand of its Creator, it *is* beautiful.

In the same way, you will not have to strive to become like Him. At the hand of your Creator, submitted to His call, you will *become* like Him—changed into His image. His yoke is easy. His burden is light.

God knows you. He knows everything about you, and He loves you still. He wants you to deeply and intimately know Him—Father God, Son Jesus, and Holy Spirit. He is not put off by anything about your personality or your past. There is nothing that disqualifies you from developing intimacy with Him. The journey I will share with you from outsider to insider, servant to friend, daughter to bride is not unlike the progression through the temple.

- OUTSIDER—The temple had Solomon's Porch, or the Court of the Gentiles, as far as those outside the faith could go.

- INSIDER—Through the Beautiful Gate (Jesus) you gained access to the Outer Court.

- SERVANT—Another gate led you to the Inner Court and past the Brazen Altar—a sacred place where priests served, offering sacrifices and gifts to God.

- FRIEND—Twelve steps brought you into the Holy Place—a place of limited access and representing greater intimacy.

- DAUGHTER—Once inside the Holy Place, you encountered the Candlestick—symbolizing light, knowledge, and guidance; the Table of Shewbread—symbolizing provision and miracles; and the Altar of Incense—symbolizing prayer. Each article in the Holy Place was filled with meaning and purpose, and those who had access to these had a special relationship with God.

- BRIDE—Lastly, a thick veil separated the Holy Place from the Holy of Holies. Only the High Priest was permitted entrance past the veil to encounter the presence of God and approach the Ark of the Covenant and the Mercy Seat—where the *Shekinah* glory of God appeared. Inside the Ark was a golden jar of manna—representing God's goodness, grace, and enduring faithfulness; Aaron's rod that budded—representing

3

Jesus and His eternal priestly authority; and the tablets of the Law—symbolizing the Lawgiver Himself. That veil was a barrier—a protection to keep those from the intimacy they were not authorized to experience. When Jesus came to earth and was crucified, that thick, heavy veil of the temple was torn in half—split top to bottom—and access to the Father and His complete presence was granted forever.[1]

Jesus longs for us to turn our hearts towards His and be fully reconciled and restored as His beloved Bride. He invites us to come with Him *Beyond the Veil* ...

Arise, my dearest,
Hurry, my darling.
Come away with me!
I have come as you have asked.
To draw you to my heart and lead you out.
For now is the time, my beautiful one.[2]

THE BRIDEGROOM KING

ENDNOTES

1. See Matthew 27:51.

2. Song of Songs 2:10, TPT.

Chapter One

GROWING UP IN BOMBAY

"Yvonne, are you coming?" my sister called from the kitchen. I hurried to finish dressing in my school uniform and went to find my breakfast of chapati and scrambled eggs prepared by our nanny, Jessy.

We were a typical middle-class Indian family living in Bombay in the 1970s. The island city has a rich history and fast-paced energy that is difficult to describe unless you have been there. There is lush vegetation contrasting the busy streets. Colonial structures are intermingled with temples, apartment buildings, churches, schools, offices ... and slums.

Our tiny apartment had just one bedroom. There was a small kitchen—too small for a table, but there was just enough room for a plain white refrigerator, a small gas cooktop, and a sink with a bit of countertop. Still, it was big enough for two people to squeeze in to cook together. The apartment had one bathroom and a living space where we gathered for meals and family life.

I lived there with my two sisters—Roshni and Queenie—my mother and father, our live-in nanny, our Pomeranian dog, and my uncle. It seems strange now to think of seven people sharing a one-bedroom apartment, but just beyond our building, we had a view of the slums where entire families shared a one-room thatched hut, so comparatively, we felt wealthy.

There were two mattresses in our bedroom that we stacked on top of each other during the daytime. At night, we pulled one mattress off to the floor. My older sister and I slept on the mattress on the bed. My mother and younger sister slept on the one we pulled off to the floor, while my father slept on a mat next to my mother. Our nanny slept on the sofa in the living room, and my uncle (or whatever relative was staying with us at the time) slept on a pallet of sheets on the living room floor.

Each morning after we got dressed, we stacked the mattresses back on top of each other, neatly folded all the sheets and bedding, and stored everything in drawers under the bed. My parents' clothing was in one metal cupboard, and the other one was ours. There was room to hang a few clothes at the top; then, there were three shelves for my sisters and me. I had the middle shelf. My sisters and I each had three pairs of shoes and a pair of gum boots for the rainy season. We had a pair of white Keds for sports, a pair of black school shoes, and one pair of sandals. These we stacked neatly beneath our cupboard, as it was unthinkable for our shoes to be out in the family living space.

In the living room, against one wall, stood three bookshelves. The shelves held books and decorations, and the bottom of each had a small cabinet covered by a door. It was here where we girls stored all our worldly possessions. I washed down my breakfast with a glass of milk, took my dishes to the sink, then retrieved my satchel of schoolbooks from my cabinet.

Jessy walked us to school each day. It was only about a ten-minute walk, which was pleasant during the dry season. But when the monsoons came, there was no way around it—even with an umbrella and the gum boots we wore, we were going to get soaked!

As we approached the building, she dropped us off under the portico with ST. ANTHONY'S spelled out in tall, free-standing red letters on top. The convent school was ivory-colored with arched windows and always seemed to be in need of a new coat of paint. My sisters and I entered through the main doors, then we separated and made our way to our classes.

The school was divided into four houses: Red House, Blue House, Green House, and Gold House. Roshni and I were not quite a year apart, and Queenie and I were separated by just twenty months. Still, Roshni was the oldest and assigned to Gold House. Queenie and I both were in Blue House. We wore the same pinafore and skirt, but our ties were different. Your tie always matched the color of your house.

Catholicism came to India in the 1600s with colonialism, and we were Catholic. Bombay was tolerant of all religions. No one evangelized each other; it was a more "live and let live" attitude. In a nation as large and diverse as India, coexistence and tolerance were vital to maintaining at least a superficial peace. Whatever religion you were born into, that was the religion you were. Perhaps this is part of the national psyche—an extension of the caste system, where Hindus are born into one of the five social classes, and this is not questioned and can never be changed. We were born Catholic—a minority religion in India. But since we were born Catholic, Catholic is what we were.

There was one solitary Protestant girl in my class, and I always used to wonder how she felt because even though the nuns taught us to be tolerant of all religions and we celebrated their religious festivals along with our Christian holidays, they were far less tolerant of other expressions of Christianity.

They were charitable toward Hinduism, Islam, Buddhism, and other religious expressions, but when it came to Christianity, they made it clear that Catholicism was the only religion—THE CHURCH—and nothing else was right. Even so, none of the children ever minded that the little girl was Protestant; we all just got along and were happy together.

My father, Gilbert, was of average height, really well-built, and had strong hands. He had dark hair and brown skin, and he could fix anything. He was not emotionally demonstrative. He didn't give out hugs or say, "I love you," or show any sort of affection. Instead, he exhibited his love for us by giving us the best shelter, food, and clothing he could provide.

Our education was *everything* to my father, so we didn't go to public school. Our convent school was the best in our area, and it cost money, but he was willing to make that sacrifice. He had been born in the southern Indian state of Karnataka in a small town called Shirva in the region of Mangalore, surrounded by mountains, streams, and lush forests filled with banyan, mango, and jackfruit trees. The second of eight children and the oldest son, my father's family was very poor. In our culture, this meant my father was responsible for the financial well-being of his parents and siblings. This always came first, and his education was not a priority.

A kind parish priest recognized my father's brightness, admired his work ethic, and intervened with my grandfather. By a miracle, my father graduated from high school.

Soon after, he was sent to Bombay (now Mumbai) to live with an uncle, more than five hundred miles away from his hometown. He wanted to work and earn money to send home to support the family. Life here was even harder. Things were unhappy in his uncle's home, and he found himself homeless, living on the streets. Father often told us tales of his youth, including how he slept with a stray dog one cold, rainy night just to stay warm. He never wanted us to take our luxuries—however small—for granted.

He worked hard at any job he could find, and a family acquaintance recommended him for an apprenticeship as a tool and die maker—a path to a trade was opened for him. Father worked tirelessly, sending money home to support his family in Mangalore. Before he was free to take any steps toward securing his own future, he first had to ensure that every one of his sisters had enough money to either be married off with a dowry or settled in life.

My mother, Philomena, was beautiful, though I doubt she ever thought of herself that way. No one in our family was ever told they were pretty—it just wasn't done. Even now, many years since I left India, when my husband tells me I am beautiful, I am almost startled by it.

Mother was born in Chembur, a quieter, greener suburb of Bombay. She was one of nine children and had been born with a deformed leg, from which God miraculously healed her. Their whole family shared an apartment not more than 220 square feet big. Whenever her mother could find work, they ate. If her mother found no work, she and her sisters were sent to visit neighbors and ask for anything spare they could take home for meals.

Mother was always busy. If I close my eyes, I can still see her sitting at her sewing machine wearing a caftan, a tape measure draped around her neck, and her long black braid falling across one shoulder. There was material all over the bed as she cut patterns and made our clothes. She sewed us frilly dresses, which we wore to church with lacy socks, made my aunties jackets with a zipper, and sewed special outfits for things like Ash Wednesday, Maundy Thursday, Good Friday, and Easter.

She and my father had an arranged marriage, decided on by the elders in the family. They started out with very little but knew the value of hard work and never shied away from it. Our needs were always met, and their work ethic and values were instilled in my sisters and me.

Mother worked for a pharmaceutical company in quality control. She was very intelligent, but this intelligence had never been encouraged. She was entrepreneurial in that she used her sewing skills to make nightgowns and other things to sell on the side for extra money. In doing this, she expressed her incredible creativity. Still, as a traditional Indian woman, her role was to be very supportive of my father and always submissive, always subjugating her desires for his and the family's needs.

We did not own a car, so while Jessy walked us to school each morning, my parents walked to the train station to get to work. Father was always tired when he got home and was often very serious with us. His standards were exacting, and you could never quite measure up. If you came in second in a race or competition, my father's brow wrinkled, and he would ask, "Why weren't you first?"

All the holidays were celebrated at our apartment—I'm not sure how we managed to fit so many people in there, but we did. On these occasions, my father would drink, laugh, and lighten up, but when it was just us, he was always serious and strict. He never had to say much; you could tell exactly what he was thinking by the look on his face. One glance told you if you were in trouble—and just how much trouble you were in!

Many Indian families view boys as an investment and girls as a liability. A boy is a future breadwinner and caregiver when his parents age. Conversely, parents are pressured to pay dowries when their daughters marry. Originally, this involved a bride receiving a gift in cash or kind from her family to help her maintain some level of independence after marriage. This practice morphed into an oppressive system that often places the family of the bride under huge financial constraints, rendering economic havoc on middle- and lower-class families. Even today, there remains a gap in the number of Indian males to females as some families abort or neglect female children resulting from these economic, cultural, and social factors.

So, most people in India would consider having three daughters and no sons highly unfortunate.

If my parents ever felt this way, they did an amazing job of shielding us from this. My mother often told us she had prayed to God to give her daughters as she had spent most of her childhood worrying about the trouble her brothers had gotten into. My father made it clear he had no preference for whether he had sons or daughters, as long as they were healthy children. We were, however, expected to be obedient, respectful, punctual, and never to do anything that would bring shame to the family's good name.

My sister Roshni was always very, very good—the model child. She excelled at school with top performance and excellent grades, which made my father very proud. I was a little less good. My grades were actually terrible. In India, everyone is multi-lingual, so I had to take classes in French, Marathi, and Hindi—and I was not very good at this. I managed to scrape by, but it was torture.

I was much better at sports. Sports was fun and an opportunity for me to excel. I was the vice-captain, which meant I got to select teams and train them for dodgeball, volleyball, and throwball. The school's houses would compete against each other, and whoever had the highest score would win the Sports Cup or the Discipline Cup. Gold House always managed to claim the Sports Cup, but Blue House proudly took the Discipline Cup.

We got our education at St. Anthony's Convent School, but Our Lady of Perpetual Succour—or OLPS as we fondly called her—was where we went for Mass. The structure is not as grandiose as Sagrada Familia in Spain or Notre Dame in Paris, but in Chembur, it was the center of all social and religious life for a robust community of Catholics in this large suburb in eastern Bombay.

The church is unlike any other building, temple, or mosque in the vicinity. It stands tall, built entirely out of a mosaic of flat stones—blue, grey, brown, and black—all held together with clean, white mortar that is interrupted only by long, narrow rectangular windows. A patchwork pattern of paving stones surrounds the building, separating it from the street and inviting you to come inside. The front entrance has a flat portico, just like St. Anthony's, but the name is etched in the stone in calligraphy instead of the towering red block letters at the school. Above the flat overhang, there is stained glass illustrating the Crucifixion, and above that, there is more stone and mortar that makes a peak topped with a cross, surrounded on both sides by taller columns of mosaic stones. It is an impressive structure.

Inside the sanctuary, the ceiling is very high in the center, with a balcony on each side and plain walls. A marble kneeling rail is used around the altar area, with more marble used for the vestibule and standing behind the tiny tabernacle that holds the bread and wine for communion. It has the traditional iconography of Catholic churches worldwide, and rows and rows of straight, hard wooden pews line the room. It is flooded with beautiful, natural light from the large expanse of windows. Standing in the sanctuary, I feel small. Everything is so expansive and high up—God is out there, way up high—and I am down here, occupying a tiny little space in the crowd.

Standing in the sanctuary, I feel small—God is out there, way up high— and I am down here, occupying a tiny little space in the crowd.

I love the rustic stone walls surrounding the church property, and the memory of the stained glass crowded with soft pink bougainvillea blooms and vines of violet morning glory stirs me still. They fight each other for space while totally unaware of the beauty their shared existence displays. This is clearly a metaphor for life here in the island city where slums and skyscrapers mingle together, each singing their strange symbiotic symphony. The walls of Our Lady of Perpetual Succour are the ultimate expression of that song.

Apart from a few hours each night, the church's heavy, brown wooden doors are always open. In addition to other services, the priests celebrate three masses daily on weekdays and as many as seven on the weekends in six different languages. For Catholics from different walks of life, OLPS was the equalizer—all were welcome here to worship side-by-side.

For my first fourteen years, every memorable experience I had took place within this group of buildings sitting heart-shaped between two streets, both called St. Anthony's Road. Now, with the surge of

Hindu nationalism in India over the last thirty years, many vestiges of Anglo-India are gradually being erased. The Bombay I grew up in is now called Mumbai. Madras is now Chennai. So, it warms my heart that these two tamarind-tree-lined arteries still miraculously bear the name St. Anthony's Road.

Roshni poked me. "Ouch!" I whispered, "What was that for?"

She rolled her eyes and pulled me to stand up beside her. As usual, I wasn't paying attention or following along. Stand. Sit. Kneel. Repeat.

Who is God? I wasn't really sure, but I suppose I believed He was there somewhere. When you needed help, you called on Him. Or you asked His mother, Mary, to pray to Him for you.

We went to Mass every Sunday. We went to Sunday School. We went to Catechism. We went to Holy Communion. Confirmation. We recited the Apostle's Creed; we said prayers we had learned by heart. We went to the Legion of Mary once a week to learn more prayers, do charity work, and volunteer.

My father did readings during Mass conducted in Konkani (his mother tongue). He was important in the church, and our family was very involved. The church was the hub, the central connection to our community, friends, and family life. You followed all the rules— and there were lots and lots and lots of rules—and checked off all those little boxes that proved you were a good Catholic. You went to Confession. Sometimes I had nothing to confess, so I would just make something up!

There was no intimacy with God. No relationship. He just was. Far away and distant. Jesus was the Son of God, and Mary was His

Mother. I knew all the rites and rituals, but it was just information to me, like arithmetic or grammar. I felt a strong connection to the people and the building, but I had no heart connection with God.

I had no intimacy with God. No relationship. He just was—I had no heart connection.

I did really look forward to Sunday dinner, though. Lunch on Sundays was different from everyday meals. It was so special that we had meat! It might be beef or chicken curry, rice with vegetables, and lentil dahl, or mincemeat kheema with potatoes and peas. There would be pickles and chapati and sometimes mango ice cream. The food was so delicious, and the apartment was fragrant with the rich aroma of curry, cardamom, coriander, and cumin.

Sometimes we ate together at the table in the living room, and sometimes we piled onto the floor in front of the television to watch *Mahabharata*—our favorite Hindu soap opera.

I belonged to this family. This family belonged to this community. This community belonged to the Church. For me, it was tribal. It was about knowing your place in the world and being accepted in it. I never thought anything about sharing my room with my parents and my sisters. I never thought about our apartment as being small. As long as I lived in this protected universe, all was right with the world.

Then my cousins from Canada came for a visit.

Outsider

Chapter Two

OUTSIDER

Awake, you who sleep,
Arise from the dead,
and Christ will give you light.[1]

FATHER GOD

My anticipation had been growing for days. Not only was Christmas approaching, but my cousins were coming all the way from Canada! Just the thought of it made me tingle with excitement. *What are they like?* I wondered. I felt very grown up and special to have such important visitors coming from abroad.

From the window of our third-floor apartment, I kept watch so I could announce their arrival the moment I saw them approach. "They're here!" I squealed, spotting them on the pavement below. "Roshni, they're here!" I repeated, jumping up and down, unable to contain my joyful energy. In a few moments, they were at the door, and there were hugs all around. Aunt Mina, Uncle Larry, Martine, Tania, and Phillip piled into our living room.

Everything about them was nice. Their clothes were freshly pressed and clean. They had lovely accessories and smelled as if they had just stepped out of the perfume section of the Duty-Free shop in the airport. My aunt's hair was stylish, and my uncle looked like an important businessman. To me, they had absolutely everything.

Usually, when family came in from out of town, they stayed with us, but my aunt and uncle had a room at the hotel—a hotel with a *swimming pool*! How I longed for the chance to swim in a swimming pool! Of course, that was out of the question, but I knew their hotel had one, and I was burning to see it. *I wonder if they'll invite me,* I thought longingly.

"Where's your room?" Tania asked me.

"My room?" I answered.

Until that moment, it had never occurred to me that I did not have my own room. I had never once thought about that question, "Where's your room?"

The question hung in the air between us awkwardly. I had seen American movies. I knew Americans were wealthy and had spacious homes and extravagant things like extra bedrooms just for their children, but it never had once entered my mind that Indian children should have one—not even those from Canada.

"Oh no," I answered reluctantly, "we don't have our own room, but let me show you where we sleep." Something uncomfortable awakened inside me. For the first time, I felt something I could not even describe, but I knew I did not have something that others did, and I didn't like the feeling.

We took our cousins into the room where we slept. They looked quizzically at the extra mattress and bedding piled on top of the bed I shared with Roshni. We showed them where we kept our clothing and shoes. I showed them "my" shelf in the bedroom armoire; then, we returned to the living room and went to the wall unit, where we kept all our school and art supplies. "We keep all our stuff in here," I said, opening my cupboard to reveal my books and supplies stacked neatly inside. I had always been proud of having my own cupboard, I knew deep down that it was much more than many had, but today it seemed small.

My father made a huge fuss over them, offering them tea and biscuits and catering to their every wish and need. It was strange seeing him so attentive. Normally, my mother would have primarily served guests, but my father seemed eager to care for them himself. Everyone visited for a time, then my uncle stood and said, "Mina, we better be getting back to the hotel," and they were soon out the door.

I rushed to the bedroom and watched them leave just as I had watched them come. I peered through the bars on the window, looking down at them as they walked away in their beautiful clothes. I caught sight of the slums and all the thatched roofs just beyond our building, and it seemed such a stark contrast to my aunt and uncle and their family's finery. Always before, when I saw the slums, it made me feel grateful for our flat. I felt well-off. My father was respected in the community and important at the church. Our home was well above average by Indian standards of living.

Today, the sight of the slums stirred something else in my little heart. Today I no longer felt wealthy. By Western standards, seven people and an animal living in a one-bedroom, one-bathroom apartment with a small kitchen and living space was something to be

> **My perspective had shifted, and that shift had brushed away my innocence of the ways of the world.**

pitied. For the first time in my life, I was awakened to lack. My perspective had shifted, and that shift had brushed away my innocence of the ways of the world.

Poverty is a strange thing to grapple with when you think about it from a global perspective. In America, you can grow up in the suburbs and never have to deal with any lack of material well-being and still be held prisoner to a mindset that is firmly rooted in poverty and lack. This same modest suburban home is a mansion in other parts of the world. Income considered "below the poverty level" in the US could sustain several families very well in many other nations.

In India, material poverty is everywhere. The slums are adjacent to skyscrapers and luxury apartments. Beggars, migrant workers, and the homeless occupy the same city blocks with highly paid tech workers and the business class. Bare feet are common. Child beggars are so much a part of the backdrop of daily life that you think nothing of them thrusting their skinny arms and dirty, eager hands toward you, hoping for a coin. You grow numb to it. You almost don't even see it.

I had never once considered our family poor, and we weren't. But when my cousins from Canada showed up with their lifestyle in such contrast to our standard of living, the seeds of an idea that we were not wealthy were planted within me.

Although my sister went swimming in the hotel pool with our cousins, my young heart was struggling to reconcile the economic differences between them and us. I now felt too awkward—maybe even slightly inferior—so I didn't join them. Their visit lasted several days, and when they went home, I decided I needed to have a little chat with God.

Imagine that! For all my religious upbringing, I had never before talked directly to God. I had recited the prayers the priests and nuns prayed, and many of those were directed to Mary, asking her to pray for us to God—not pray to God for ourselves. I had not developed any sort of relationship with God beyond believing He existed and that I would get in trouble if I broke His rules. But my mind was now troubled. Instinctively, I knew that when you had a really deep question about life, you were supposed to go to God with that.

That afternoon after school, I stole away, perched myself on the bedroom window ledge, and stared down through the wrought iron bars. The street below was busy, and I was struck by the diverse group of people who made their way past the building we lived in. Unsure of exactly how to pray on my own, I finally just plunged in.

"God, why *them* and not *me*?" I asked.

Silence.

"Why did my *cousins* end up in Canada and not *me*?"

Silence.

Hot tears stung my eyes, "Why was *she* born into that family and not *me*?"

Silence.

I wiped my eyes and sniffled, "God, why does *she* have her own room ... and not *me*?"

More silence.

I let out a deep sigh, feeling sorry for myself, "And why does *she* get to travel all over the world and not *me*?"

More silence.

Just then, my one-sided conversation with God was interrupted.

Something caught my attention. A young child walked by, homeless. Naked. He had not one stitch of clothing on him, and there was no adult nearby who seemed to know or care that he was wandering the streets alone or why he was naked.

The silence was heavy.

I watched the small child patter aimlessly down the street. He had nothing. Absolutely nothing.

My prayer had felt one-sided and fruitless, but now I know it was God speaking to me through this impoverished child. From my limited perspective, my Canadian cousins had everything. After all, if they could afford for their children to have their own bedroom and their family could afford to travel all over the world, what more could possibly be had? All I had to my name was my little shelf in the bedroom armoire and my little shelf in the living room wall unit. The furthest I had ever been away from home was when we traveled to my dad's village in Mangalore to visit my grandparents.

That trip was not a stylish flight to a modern airport, but a torturous twenty-four-hour bus ride through some of the most perilous mountain passes in the Western Ghats of India—literally a cliffhanger. My sisters and I had so much motion sickness we vomited most of the way there. When we were smaller, we traveled the entire way on my parent's laps to avoid paying for additional seats. I had never once thought of it as a luxury or a blessing.

But to our cousins in Mangalore, *we* were the wealthy ones. We were the big city kids coming to visit the village. To them, we had everything. They lived in mud houses. We lived in a "high-rise" apartment (three stories). We went to a nice convent school. My parents had well-paying blue-collar jobs, and being able to afford a vacation away from Mumbai's hustle and bustle to visit the Mangalore countryside was extravagant. In truth, our lifestyle was well above average in India, but after my cousins from Canada visited, I was fixated on what we didn't have and couldn't do.

Now, this naked child brought into stark reality what poverty really looked like.

"Why *him* and not *you*?" I thought I heard.

"I guess I have it good. Very good. I suppose I shouldn't be complaining. I'm sorry," I replied.

My father had always worked hard to give us the best opportunities he could afford. He wanted to give us a better life. The population in India is so massive that it is difficult to stand out. Hundreds or even thousands of people may apply for a single job, so it is very competitive. My dad began to feel like there were just not enough opportunities available for his girls. My mom's sister, two brothers, and cousins had all moved to Canada to raise their families, and in 1981, when my father went to visit them, he began thinking about migrating there, and he got the lay of the land. Some time after he returned, he applied for immigration status, but his application was denied.

My dad did not give up, and we later applied again, only this time, my Aunt Mina and Uncle Larry sponsored us, pledging to take care of us. This time we were approved to migrate. I still remember our whole family traveling an hour away by bus to get a physical, which we all passed. My father took us to a restaurant to celebrate—which was a *very* big deal. We never ate out other than at our aunties' and uncle's homes. It was such an adventure!

We began making our preparations. My parents helped Jessy secure a new nanny position with an uncle in Bangalore, but we were unsure what to do with Shebu, our Pomeranian. I couldn't imagine leaving her behind, and it was as if she knew something was up. A few months after we were approved to leave, Shebu got an infection and died, so in the end, she left us.

It was 1991 before we finally moved to Montreal. I am not sure how my parents felt about leaving India behind, but to me, it felt like a grand holiday. The "foreverness" of our departure and the magnitude of our move had not yet sunk in. My 10 Standard Exams were just around the corner, and when I learned we were leaving before I would have to take them, I was ecstatic! I had never been a very good student, and I had such fear of failing that leaving seemed like a great escape!

We didn't leave until July, a few months before my fourteenth birthday. My father made us begin the school year in India anyway, but I skated along without the pressure to perform and pass exams.

When we finally arrived in Montreal, it was as if I had stepped through a portal to an entirely new world. It was completely unlike anything I had ever known. There was a new culture, and they spoke a different language. My father leased an apartment on the twelfth floor—this time, we made our home in a spacious, two-bedroom, two-bathroom flat which was very comfortable. My parents, at last, had their own bedroom, and my sisters and I shared the other one. And our building had a *swimming pool*—I was in heaven! In the beginning, we all went to work for Aunt Mina and Uncle Larry's import business until we could get situated with something more permanent. The high-rise penthouse complex my dad chose had been suggested to us by Aunt Mina because it was a short 10-minute walk to their place, and they were literally the only people we knew.

Working for my Aunt and Uncle was my first part-time job, and I felt very grown up. They sold costume jewelry, leggings, bags, scarves, t-shirts, belts, and other treasures from all over the world. Our family helped out in their boutique, worked in their warehouse, and we were all hands on deck for the annual sidewalk sale on the busy, bustling St.-Laurent and Prince Arthur Boulevards in Montreal's trendy district, the Plateau Mont-Royal. It felt more like play than work to me as I imagined the warehouse was Aladdin's Cave and the boutique was a far-off, exotic shop. I honestly don't know how we would have survived were it not for their generosity, and to this day, I remain humbly grateful.

Converting our savings from Rupees to Canadian Dollars was a shock. Everything here was *so* expensive. The rent was high. Food was costly. Clothing. All of it was astonishing. Intimidating but also thrilling. Alas, the cold, hard reality set in, and my self-esteem took a hit. I was an immigrant. An Indian immigrant. A second-class citizen in this luxurious world. We looked and spoke and dressed and ate differently than everyone around us. I felt like an outsider. Some of the locals were not very kind, and as I started school, my confidence was shaken.

Alas, the cold, hard reality set in ... I felt like an outsider.

Private school was far too expensive, so it was out of the question. Because we were immigrants, we had to go to a French public school—École Secondaire Saint-Luc—where we studied French and where all our classes were taught in French. At first, it was an adventure to take a bus to the Metro station, where we rode the subway, then caught another bus to get to school. The first snow was very exciting. But as winter wore on, my excitement waned. It grew colder than I imagined was even possible, and soon that trip back and forth to school became abysmal.

In India, we had many extracurricular activities, and I excelled in sports while being only an average student. (Which, to my father, was below average.) Although we had art class and gym in this new school, there were no other activities to distract me from my schoolwork, and I excelled.

Math class had been incredibly difficult back home. I always felt behind. There, on an exam, you were given 100 questions to answer in one hour without a calculator. Here, we were given twenty-five questions to answer in three hours, and you were encouraged to use a calculator. The first time I was confused because I finished my work in only forty-five minutes. I looked around, and everyone else was still working diligently, so I thought I must have done something wrong.

I took my test up to the teacher's desk to turn it in. She looked at me over the top of her glasses as I stood before her and said, "Here, I'm done."

"Are you sure?" she asked. "Perhaps you should go and look it over."

"I did," I answered. "I'm done."

Dubiously, she took the papers from my hand and said, "Okay, then let me just correct it right here."

I stood there, watching her in disbelief as she went question by question down the page. She made one tiny mark and looked up at me, smiling as she wrote "99" on the top.

I took the paper and went back to my desk, dumbfounded. For the first time in my life, I thought, *I'm intelligent. I am book-smart. Academic. I am not just good at art and athletics—I have a brain!* And something on the inside of me began to believe in myself.

Our school had many French Quebec children attending, but their classes were kept separate from ours. Many in Quebec wanted to separate from Canada and be their own country. If you didn't speak French to them, they wouldn't answer you, even if they knew English. The message was clear that we were not wanted there. You had to prove yourself in order to be accepted, and if you had nothing to offer that they wanted, you were a drain on society. They didn't need you and had no interest in rolling out the red carpet to make you feel welcome. So once again, I knew I didn't belong. I was an outsider.

In my classes, all the immigrant children from more than sixty nations were grouped together, all at different ages and academic levels. Out of necessity, there was a great deal of self-directed study to complete assignments. I had to work very hard because I knew very little French, but with no sports and not being involved yet in the community or a church, I threw myself into my studies. By year's end, I had caught up with my older sister, and we started out the next year in the same grade. My sister was very intelligent. She had always excelled at academics, so being put in the same class with her served to reinforce this new, fledgling belief that I was smart.

Aunt Mina and Uncle Larry were very generous, and I hardly ever remember them saying no to us. If one of my sisters or I wanted to purchase something from them, they gave us a deeply discounted price. This gracious display should have made me more grateful, but that terrible demon of comparison caused me to rationalize that they were generous because they were wealthy. I am ashamed to admit that this was often my justification for stealing a few dollars from the cash register, imagining that they could afford this easily and it would not make a difference to them.

I had much to learn. Even back in India as a younger child, I often walked out of a shop with a stolen piece of candy. I had no good reason for this, and my parents certainly did not raise me this way.

They worked exceptionally hard to give us the best of everything they could afford. They sacrificed for us and stretched every penny, but I was never satisfied. Whatever we had, I wanted something more. So, I always felt like it wasn't a big deal to take something so small—almost as though I deserved it because only our most basic needs were being met, and we had few luxuries. Even a small piece of candy was extravagant, and I resented that I couldn't have it, so I justified helping myself. It seemed so small and insignificant, just as a few dollars gone missing from my aunt's cash register. Our standard of living had improved dramatically, but that core desire of wanting more was still unmet. I didn't realize then that I was struggling to fill a God-shaped hole in my heart with things—things that could never come close to replacing Him.

My parents soon found employment, but I worked for my aunt for a year. It was a good experience for me, and she was kind enough to use her influence and get an opportunity for my sister and me to interview with the manager at a McDonald's restaurant close to our home. I was hired for a probationary period of three months, and I was not a very good cashier. I was almost let go, but the manager was of Indian descent and had a connection to my aunt, so grace was extended to me.

At the end of my probation, I had learned a great deal and was much improved. In time, I was promoted to the position of crew trainer. I was a dependable, hard worker, I liked earning money, and I made myself available for any shift. I even bought a pager so they could contact me to fill in for any shift. While not the job of my dreams, it taught me much about servanthood. I learned to clean as I went along, to be efficient, and get people in and out as quickly as possible. I learned to be aware of people's needs, and I learned that sales was a service. McDonald's had policies, processes, and procedures for every aspect of every operation. They drilled the up-sell and suggestive sale into me, and I still use these tools today.

There wasn't a lot of room for creative expression. I was told what to do and how to do it. I followed those instructions to the letter and did it as fast as possible. You know that joke about the milkshake or ice cream machine always being broken? That wasn't a joke to me. It was my opportunity to become indispensable. I learned how to fix it, mastering the art of taking it apart, cleaning it, and putting it back together. Anytime they had a problem, they didn't call maintenance; they called me!

My job and financial independence became idols to me. Though still in high school, education was no longer a priority. I was a teenage immigrant earning her own money. I constantly converted my minimum wage salary from Canadian dollars into Rupees and convinced myself I was swimming in wealth!

My job and financial independence became idols to me ... the drive to earn money engulfed me. It became my means of proving myself to the world.

I acted as if I had no parents. No family. No home. No inheritance. I had not yet learned even the concept of an "orphan spirit," but I had one. I was dollar-driven. If I made the money, then I could determine how to spend the money, and I spent it as quickly as I earned it. I thought this was financial freedom. I believed if I could make enough money then I would not have to depend on my parents (or anyone else). If I could buy whatever I wanted without even looking at the price tag, then I would have "made it." The drive to earn money engulfed me. It became my means of proving myself to the world.

When our lease was up, my father found a new apartment, much less luxurious, in a less affluent part of town, and more reasonable in rent. Of course, this made sense financially, but it underscored that "you don't belong here" belief in my heart. If we were making more money, we could have stayed at the nicer location. So, money became the answer for belonging.

I felt more and more on the outside at school as I worked more and more shifts, often late into the night. I didn't know I was hurting on the inside. I didn't know my hunger was for God, and I vented this dissatisfaction into becoming the class clown. I was mischievous, and my pranks terrorized my classmates and tormented my teachers. Making people laugh became a way to fit in, and my popularity grew as my practical jokes gained a reputation. Before long, I found ways to pass my tests and get others to write my papers for me. I wasn't dull; I had decided that making the money was smarter than making the grades. Working was a better use of my time than studying.

Miraculously, though I never did become fluent in French, I graduated from French high school. At last, I was able to take college classes in English! By this time, I had been at McDonald's for three years, and I was up for a promotion. I knew I was going to get it. I had no doubt. When I was overlooked for this position, I was deeply hurt. I had devoted myself wholly to this job and put everything else on the back burner. I was so offended that I was ready to quit, and I almost did. My father wisely advised me against quitting a job without having another one already lined up, so I waited.

I worked hard, and I waited. I no longer belonged—not even here at McDonald's. No matter how hard I tried, I did not fit in. I wrapped "outsider" around my identity and decided I would have to make my own way in the world.

ENDNOTE

1. Ephesians 5:14, NKJV.

Insider

Chapter Three

INSIDER

Arise, my dearest.
Hurry, my darling.
Come away with me!
I have come as you have asked
to draw you to my heart and lead you out.
For now is the time, my beautiful one.[1]

THE BRIDEGROOM KING

My mother had a sister named Theresa. In 1975, she had set the all-India record in the high jump. After that, she entered Khalsa College in Mumbai, where she worked hard—running in knee-deep water to strengthen her muscles and trained with Sikh male runners. She excelled both as a long-distance runner and high jumper, and gained some fame as newspapers dubbed her the "Queen of the Track." She worked afternoons for the Western Railway Board in exchange for their sponsorship of her to the Olympics. Late one night in her parent's (my grandparent's) bedroom, Theresa had an encounter with God. She gave Him her life. She relinquished her dreams of being an Olympic athlete and responded to God's call by choosing to join a local convent and enter novitiate training as a nun. The Loreto Convent is where the famous Nobel Prize-winning Mother Teresa spent twenty years before starting Missionaries of Charity.

One afternoon, by an incredibly unlikely and miraculous circumstance, Mother Teresa visited Loreto, and she and my aunt met each other. Years later, my Aunt Theresa had the opportunity to walk the streets of Calcutta with Mother Teresa and see the miracle power of God at work. She gave herself fully to serving God in the Roman Catholic Church and was made headmistress, then principal of the Lucknow Intermediate College.

But the Lord kept speaking to her—calling to her—and calling her out of Catholicism. There she was, young and dedicated, busy about the Lord's business and basking in the kind of affirmation that work gave her, but God was inviting her into something new and different. It was a season of great unrest for her.

While this was happening for my Aunt Theresa, my Aunt Christine (my mother's older sister) was living outside of India. Christine spoke eight languages and was an international businesswoman. She once sold ships and had worked for the United Nations based in Germany, where she settled in as a single mom to raise her daughter. It just so happened that her neighbor was Reinhard Bonnke—the famous German-American Pentecostal evangelist. She became friends with him and his family, and he led her to salvation. After that, she gave up her career and went to England to study at Elim Pentecostal Church College in London. One night, she called my aunt and shared a vision from God about her leaving the convent and taking His word to the ends of the earth. That phone call set off a series of confirmations that led Theresa to leave the Catholic Church and embrace a new adventure with God after serving thirteen and a half years as a nun.

While both sisters were beginning to explore a deeper relationship with God, my mother also began to feel a hunger for something more. Aunt Theresa moved to Peterborough in Ontario to attend Bible college, so we saw more of her. Aunt Christine came for a visit simultaneously, and the three had long talks together. My mother's heart was ripe for the harvest, and she, too, invited Jesus to come to live there as her Lord and Savior. She learned that Jesus was the great High Priest and that He alone had the power to forgive sin and wash her clean, presenting her to the Father as acceptable and righteous.

This is a fundamental break with Catholicism, where a human priest is inserted between a person and God. So, my mother began to search for an evangelical church where she could grow in the faith. My father was considerably less enthused about this development. Still, while her sisters were there visiting, and it was apparent they wanted to visit a non-Catholic church, my practical father looked for one that was not far from our apartment.

Though he did not attend with us, he drove my mom and her two sisters, along with me and my two sisters, to attend a service on a Friday night. We pulled up to a church building that had a sign out front indicating it was a Presbyterian church, but we did not go up the front steps or through the main door as you would for a Catholic church. This was very strange to me, and I didn't know what to expect.

Instead, we parked on a side street where we could see a fellowship hall behind the church building, which seemed to be where people were going. So, we went there too, entering the hall through a side door.

There was no stained glass.

There was no carpet.

There were no statues.

There was no big cross with Jesus hanging from it.

It was a multi-purpose room where people could play basketball on the concrete floor. All the wooden beams were made of dark wood, and the windows were up high and made of frosted glass. It was night, so no light came through them. What light there was available was dim, but I could see neat rows of brown metal folding chairs. There were about a hundred, I guessed.

I felt awkward and uncomfortable, unsure of what to do, but my Aunt Christine walked in like she owned the place, greeting people and shaking their hands. Aunt Maggie was also friendly and outgoing, and they seemed completely at home. My mother was much more shy, and I hid in the shadow of my aunts, watching, listening, and taking it all in. There were only about thirty people in the room, lots of teens and young adults who all knew each other, so we really stuck out as newcomers. I was glad there were six of us, and I felt great relief when we finally sat down in a row of chairs nearer to the back.

The music began. There were drums and an electric guitar, and the pastor's wife led the singing. I had no expectations, no pre-judgments—it was all so new—I stood as a neutral observer. Instead of hymn books, there was an overhead projector—like at school—and someone put up transparencies with the words to the songs being cast up on a big screen so we could follow along. Even though I didn't know these songs, the words rang true, so I tried my best to sing along. There was no priest. No sacraments. No kneeling up and down, and in the absence of ritual, there was something fresh and organic in the people's participation. It felt spontaneous and unrehearsed.

I had only known strict formality in my approach to God. This informal setting took me off guard. One of the musicians made a mistake, bringing laughter from the congregation as they just stopped and started over again. It felt more like we were in someone's living room instead of a sanctuary. It was like being among family.

My eyes were wide with wonder, and I noticed a young man singing passionately with his hands raised high above his head. The authenticity of his praise struck me profoundly. This was very real. Very moving. I had never seen a young person in the Catholic church ever invested like that. This guy was clearly moved by something, and his response was so pure that it caught my attention.

There was something fresh and organic in the people's participation—it felt spontaneous and unrehearsed. I had only known strict formality in my approach to God.

This experience made a deep impression on me.

My aunts both left a few days later, and my mother announced that she wanted to begin attending that fellowship regularly. This created some tension in our home, as my father was a devoted Catholic and had no desire to go elsewhere. He did not like the idea of my mother going to church without him, and he liked it even less that he would have to attend church alone without her.

I was too young to understand the deeper roots of the conflict. Since we had arrived in Canada, everything had changed for my father. In India, he was a highly respected member of the community. He was an important man in the parish and participated there as someone to be looked up to and respected. There he had earned a better-than-average living and provided well for his wife and daughters, sending them to a convent school and giving them a good education.

After arriving in Canada, the Catholic church he had chosen for us to attend was very close to our apartment, just as our church had been close to our apartment in India. I am sure it was chosen for the convenience of being so nearby. Partly for the ease, but I think more so we could be very involved, just as we had back in Bombay. It was in this Canadian church where I had my Confirmation. I was proud to share this milestone with my older sister. In India, we had done our first Holy Communion together, and here, we had gone to Catechism classes together, completed our five requirements together, and were confirmed together. For me, it was just about checking the boxes to be a good daughter and a good Catholic. It wasn't much different than getting my six-month cleanings at the dentist or yearly physicals. I felt nothing.

But it made my father incredibly proud to be a Catholic and to have his daughters raised as good Catholics. When we had our Confirmation, he threw a big party. My Uncle Gerald came and stood by me as a sponsor. It was a memorable day.

Now all of us worked jobs and earned our own money. Of course, we still lived in the apartment my father provided, but we no longer had to ask him for spending money. We bought our own clothes, paid for our own school, and often even ate out at restaurants, away from the family table. We needed him less. He was not such an important figure in this community. Few knew him. Now, my mother no longer wanted to remain by his side in the Catholic church. I imagine he must have felt abandoned and betrayed. His manhood was challenged as we flexed our independence and made more and more decisions on our own—with or without his blessing or approval.

In India, he had really been somebody. Here, I think he felt small.

My mother and sisters began regularly attending Bethel, the Pentecostal church that met in the fellowship hall of the Presbyterian church. All this created an underlying irritation in my father, though He never forbade my mother to go to this church. I used the chaos at home as an opportunity to accept even more shifts and make more money by skipping church, hoping they would not notice.

Being a good and loyal husband and father, my dad didn't want my mom or sisters to walk or take mass transit to services. Perhaps it was pride; I don't know, but he would drop them off, go to Mass, then come back to pick them up. Though he took them, he was not approving. His communication grew increasingly passive-aggressive. When one of us did something or said something wrong, he would say, "Oh, is *that* what they taught you at that church?"

It was okay with him for us to work until midnight. It was okay with him if we were at the library studying for exams until midnight. We could work 30-40 hours on top of our classes, and that was okay, but try hanging out with the youth group at a supervised event past 9:00 pm, and he would get angry.

My dad had never been an affectionate man; he showed his love for us by providing the best he could for us. As we got older, we argued more and more. I could not please him, no matter how hard I tried. He had grown up in difficult circumstances. I am sure he never heard his father say the words, "I love you" or "I'm proud of you." Being sent far away so young to earn money and send it back home must have been extremely difficult. Nothing had ever been given to him; he had earned everything on his own. And to this day, he has difficulty receiving anything from us. He won't take anything he has not earned.

Still, he was a man of high moral character with a solid work ethic and loved us the best way he knew. He cared that we grew up well. So, he noticed that I was not attending either church. I had a bicycle, so I biked to work—now on Sundays, too.

One afternoon, he sat me down and said, "Yvonne, let's have a conversation."

I dreaded that prospect; sure I had done something wrong I was about to be in trouble for. But instead, my dad said, "I see that you are not going to church with me, and you are not going to church with your mom. You need to decide where you want to go. You must go somewhere. Going nowhere is not an option."

I looked at him, feeling my paycheck dwindle.

"But I …" I began.

"No, you need to pick one, Yvonne."

I knew my father was relieved that we all worked and made money because everything in Canada was so expensive, and our paychecks helped out with the finances.

"But I can make more money if I take these extra shifts," I bargained.

"No, you will not be working at that time. You must choose. You will either go to church with your mother or with me, but you will go somewhere."

I chose Bethel. It seemed more fun.

My father's advice rang true. I knew he was right about going to church and not working all the time. And now that I was struggling so much with wanting to quit my job at McDonald's, his advice in this matter was just as true. It was not wise to leave a job before you had a new one secured. Besides, I was now very used to the money I was making, and I spent it so quickly I couldn't afford a gap in pay. So, I stayed at my post at McDonald's, resenting every minute of every shift.

I was angry.

Frustrated.

I worked very hard and always had top employee reviews and praise from customers. I believed if you worked hard, showed up for extra shifts, and did everything you were supposed to do, that meant you would get promoted. But instead, a woman who was sleeping with the manager got the job—*my* job, the one I deserved. The injustice stung.

Deeply.

I should not have needed to do anything else. Hard work should have been enough. This young lady frequently came in late or called out sick. She neglected her responsibilities, passing them on to others or just leaving them undone. When she was promoted to shift leader, she would become my boss—*over me!* The situation was impossible. Each time I saw her or when she just passed by me behind the counter, my anger boiled. I was furious.

I put on a brave face, unwilling to give her the satisfaction of even knowing I was bothered. I worked that much harder— smiled at the customers, cleaned up as I went along, upsold, went the extra mile in every way—but I was steaming. The more I meditated on the injustice, the more it riled me up until my soul was in a downward spiral of aggravation and self-pity. I had no framework yet for taking these thoughts captive, no grid for processing them with the Holy Spirit or praying for my "enemy." Without these tools or understanding, I shoved

I had no framework yet for taking these thoughts captive, no grid for processing them with the Holy Spirit, so I shoved my feelings down deep inside.

my feelings down deep inside. I wanted to prove them wrong. Make them regret their poor decision and be vindicated.

Each day, I wanted to quit. Everything in me wanted to walk out, but I would not give them the satisfaction. My responsibility gene was so stretched out that I wouldn't leave them short-staffed or have customers go unserved. I kept my brave face on, swearing I could handle it, but my heart got harder and harder.

I no longer belonged.

I didn't belong at work. I didn't belong at either church. I didn't even really belong at home anymore—in that odd space between childhood and adulthood where you don't quite fit in either world.

I was ready to stop being an outsider. I wanted to belong.

I started looking for a new job, and my dad kept his eyes and ears open as well. While conversing with someone at the local bank, it came up that I was looking for employment. The woman told him, "We are looking for a teller; why don't you send your daughter in for an interview?"

Later that week, I sat down with the woman. She began, "I see here you have been employed for some time at McDonald's while in high school. Everyone knows you aren't going to work there to make a career out of it; you just work there while you are in school. Are you interested in a career in banking?"

Now, I SHOULD have said, "Oh yes, absolutely!" But I had no training on how to interview properly, so I laughed and responded, "No. I just want a job here, so I am not at McDonald's anymore. I just want to make as much money as possible while I'm in school. I plan to be a dentist."

I had no real interest in dentistry, mind you, but I thought dentists made a lot of money because everyone has teeth, so everyone needs a dentist. I had a mouthful of cavities that kept our dentist—both in India and Canada—quite busy. My father had complained about how much my cavities cost, so I knew dentists made a lot of money. I wanted to make a lot of money.

Thankfully, the lady hired me anyway, and I began working as a part-time bank teller. After just three weeks on the job, I was taken in by a con artist. The fraudulent client cashed a bad check for $3,000— which was a lot of money! I was mortified. I was sure I would be fired for not spotting the scheme. Ultimately, I was not fired, but my ability to trust people went even lower. After my experience at McDonald's, I already thought people were shady, and getting taken for a ride here at my new job made me double down on being wary of anyone I didn't know.

Growing up in India, we were raised to trust no one except for a few close family members. Even extended family members might be outside the circle of trust. There was constant crime surrounding us, so I grew up with gates and bars covering our doors and windows. Distrust was part of the landscape of my everyday living, and I did not realize how much it impacted my mental landscape. I trusted no one at my counter, and I became a super sleuth. Nothing got past me. Everything was by the book—no exceptions!

The McDonald's customer service training and the art of the upsell paid off. Not only was my drawer always correct to the penny, and no one got anything past me, but I was good at selling additional products and services to bank customers. I also spoke a few languages, and I was eager to fill in for anyone who was ill or vacationing. As before, I gave everything to my job. Within six months, I was promoted to Customer Service Representative, and I began to see a new path opening before me.

If banking was the path to making money, then so be it.

I was completely ignorant of my goals, my passion, my purpose, or any sense of the calling on my life. I had been raised to work hard and never bring any "shame to the family name." Banking was a respectable career choice, one my father approved, which was an added bonus for me. It met no resistance at home.

I was accepted here. Valued. At last, I felt like I belonged—like an insider. People respected me at the bank. I was even called to fill in for people at other branches around Montreal.

At last, my identity as an "immigrant" was no longer the most defining thing about me. I was dependable. Reliable. I could be counted on to do excellent work, and I was gaining a reputation as a valuable and trusted member of the banking community. This sense of acceptance and financial freedom was a huge motivator for me. Life was good. I was making good money while going to college, now studying finance to further a banking career. Of course, I continued to spend it as fast as I earned it—but I felt like I was on my way to success as I had defined it.

I kept my promise to my father, and the bank was closed on Sundays anyway, so I started attending services at Bethel regularly. I was always moved while I was there. There was light and joy and freedom. I never walked an aisle or responded to an altar call, but every time there was an invitation to pray the sinner's prayer, I said it while sitting in my seat. I told myself, "I do believe Jesus died for our sins. I accept Him as my Lord and Savior. I don't need a priest, and I don't need to walk down any aisle, either. I accept Him. That's that."

I did accept Him. I was saved, and God began working in my life. My heart was more and more open to things of the Spirit, and the sermons were beginning to awaken hunger in my soul. I reached for God—hesitantly. I wanted a real relationship with Him.

I reached for God—hesitantly. I wanted a real relationship with Him.

Then I would go home. There was such a dichotomy there since my parents were not united in their faith. There was a tangible heaviness in our home—a perpetual conflict. There I was under my father's authority. In India, we are taught to honor and respect our parents as a lifelong duty. For as long as they are living, you honor and obey. So, my spirit would be awakened at church; then, when I went home, it was like it shut down under a dark cloud. I felt like I took two steps forward at church only to take three steps backward at home, and I grew frustrated. It was a difficult environment in which to grow.

But I kept going. For years, I attended services while going to college and working at the bank. I got involved and made friends, and my sense of belonging deepened. In 1997, I met Paul. Paul was British and had come to Canada to work with a cousin in the car business. One of his friends attended Bethel and invited him to our church. He walked in wearing a tie, and I thought, *What in the world is wrong with this guy?* We were a collection of about thirty young people in our jeans and sneakers, and here was this British guy in a dress shirt and tie! Even though our group was relatively small, we still had smaller cliques within the larger group. Paul had his friends, and I had mine. We didn't really interact with each other.

After he had been there for some time, he invited the entire young adult group to his place. He lived on the top floor of a duplex, and when I walked in, I was impressed by his apartment. I already knew him as a strong believer who loved the Lord. He was bold and direct, and having been baptized in the Holy Spirit; there was something powerful about the way he lived life. He made spaghetti and meatballs for the entire group, which caught my attention. He was young and attractive. He had a nice place all to himself. He was confident and secure and wasn't afraid to cook food for and entertain thirty people!

That night, he asked for everyone's emails so he could stay connected, and mine was among them. He started sending out emails to everyone with comments about a Bible study or to share some revelation he had from scripture. Every now and again, I would respond to one, and in time we began having random conversations through email. We still did not talk to each other in person at church, but we were getting to know each other via the world wide web.

Rex, a mutual friend, kept trying to set us up to date, but I wasn't really interested. Paul was strait-laced and a nice guy. I was more attracted to bad boys—he was just too goody-goody for me.

On New Years' Day 1999, my phone rang. It was Paul. "Hello there, what are you up to?" he asked.

"Not much; my parents have gone to Toronto," I replied.

"I am going to Sister Eileen's house to grocery shop for her," he said. Sister Eileen was a member of our church. She was a sweet seventy-year-old lady and a born-again nun. Paul was helping buy her groceries and making sure she had food in her house.

"Oh?" I replied, "Do you need any help?" I gave him an opportunity.

"Oh, no thanks," he said, "I'm all set!"

He's so dumb, I thought, *I just opened the door wide, and he did not catch my clue.* "Oh, okay then," I said, "Happy New Year … goodbye," and I hung up the phone.

Two minutes later, the phone rang again. It was Paul.

"Oh no—no, no, no—would you like to come shopping with me? That would be great. In fact, I could really use your help!"

I laughed and said, "Okay, sure."

Not long after, he picked me up, and we went to Canadian Tire—sort of like a Sam's Club or Costco. There was Paul, like a man on a mission. He was focused. Intense. Bold. Confident. Loud. I was shy and reserved. I was carrying around a lot of baggage that had my self-esteem pretty low. Paul talked to everyone, called the cashiers by name, and had no trouble asking anyone and everyone for help locating items. It was too much! I walked slowly behind him, thinking, *Oh, wow!*

We loaded up the car and went to Sister Eileen's. She lived in an upstairs apartment, so it took several trips to carry up laundry detergent, potatoes, rice, and all the groceries. I stood at the top of the landing, holding the door open as Paul brought the items up the stairs. Sister Eileen said to Paul, "Is this your girlfriend?"

I froze, thinking, *The less I say, the better.*

Paul answered confidently, "Yes!" but explained nothing.

I walked back down to his car, puzzled. We didn't talk about it at all. We did not mention that he had just told Sister Eileen I was his girlfriend. Instead, he asked, "Do you want to get something to eat?"

Without waiting for an answer, he continued, "I know this great Greek place! Marvin's. They have the best lamb chops ever. You'll love them!"

I love to eat, so I said, "Sure."

We were seated, and I started looking at the menu. I really enjoy browsing menus. I like to see what they have—everything they have so I can decide what I want to eat right now and maybe what I might like to return for to eat in the future. But before I could begin, Paul collected my menu and his and said, "Don't worry, I'll order for us."

Excuse me, I thought. I am pretty independent, and I wasn't sure about this. Besides, I needed to see the prices. I planned on paying for my own food, and my father had JUST rescued me from a $3,000 credit card bill. I was an adult at 21, but with my father's intervention, I was on a slim $20/week allowance from my own bank account with my own money so I could resolve my debt from overspending. I wanted to make sure I was going to order inside my budget, so this really took me off guard.

The waiter approached our table, and Paul began talking to him like they were long-lost friends. He said, "We'll have one lamb chop. One salad. One order of fries and two drinks, please."

I'm hungry, I thought. *One order? Will it be enough?* I squirmed, uncomfortable.

Sure enough, a few minutes later, the waiter reappeared carrying a platter of food that was so abundant it could have fed four people! It was delicious. I savored every bite of that lamb.

The check came, and Paul scooped it up before there was any chance for awkwardness. He paid the bill and left a generous tip.

So—not a loser, I mused.

"Want to have dinner again tomorrow?" he asked as he dropped me off.

Apparently, we were now boyfriend and girlfriend.

My sense of belonging grew. The more Paul and I got to know each other, the more of an insider I became. He let me in, and I let him in.

He was expressive about everything. He told me I was beautiful. He told me, "I love you," and made me feel so precious. Bit by bit, he was beginning to help me renew my mind. My esteem began to grow, and I was changing more and more into who I was created to be. That April, we got engaged. The contrast between time spent with Paul and time spent with my father became difficult to ignore. One night, I got into a huge argument with my father.

Originally, we were going to get married the following August so I could finish college first, but after this heated argument, I knew the only way to get out of my house was to get married. The next morning, I called Paul and asked, "Do you want to get married this summer instead of next?"

He said, "Yes!" So that August, I walked down the aisle and became his bride.

Once out of my father's house, the black cloud lifted. I no longer felt like I advanced when I was away and retreated when I was home. I was free to grow. Paul nurtured this growth in me, and I responded to his tenderness. I tasted freedom.

One afternoon in our first year of marriage, I got into a car accident. I expected Paul to be very angry with me. My father certainly would have been. In fact, when I told my dad, he was more concerned about the car and how much damage I had done. When I told Paul, he was concerned only about me. When I fretted over the car, he said, "Sweetheart, that is just plastic and metal; we can fix that." I expected anger, but I got only grace.

Life was very, very different.

On my journey from outsider to insider, I had a lot of questions, though I wasn't yet ready to ask them. I did not understand the kingdom of God or how it worked, but God's eternal plans for my

> **I had always operated in pride. Now I was in a place of surrender. I was ready to become a servant in God's house.**

life were definitely in motion. I had always operated in pride. Now I was in a place of surrender. For the first time, it was okay that I didn't know everything or understand; I could trust. I just volunteered, showing up to serve and learning that God was working all things for my good. I began to pursue Him gently and steadily—not yet fully and completely given to Him—but willing to walk the next step and the next on my journey.

I was ready to become a servant in God's house.

ENDNOTE

1. Song of Songs 2:10, TPT.

Servant

Chapter Four

SERVANT

The season has changed,
the bondage of your barren winter has ended,
and the season of hiding is over and gone.
The rains have soaked the earth ...[1]

THE BRIDEGROOM KING

In the early days of my marriage to Paul, I felt more like an insider than at any time in my life. I belonged to God. I belonged to Paul. I belonged to the family at Bethel and even at the bank where I worked. I was finding my place in the world and beginning to peel back the layers as the desire to discover my identity was awakened. My relationship with God was far from perfect, but my journey into the Kingdom was underway. At last, I felt like I was heading in the right direction, and I actively responded to the Lord's leading.

When I received my training at McDonald's, I learned the value of service. As I began to embrace life as a believer, I responded with service. It was a language I knew and understood. I was trained to serve. I was faithful to prioritize attending Bethel, and I began to sense God's Spirit prompting me to do things. Slowly, I learned how to distinguish His voice from all others and how to obey—first in small things, then gradually with larger ones. God always blessed the work of my hands, and it was easy to see the correlation between willing obedience and God's blessings. It was the dawn of an amazing new chapter in my life.

Now, it may sound very spiritual to say, "I was a devoted servant of God," but remember, I was driven to earn money and prove my worth by my balance sheet. In India, only the very poor are servants. Those with no education and no other advantages or choice become servants to the rich or middle class. I grew up middle class, so we had a live-in nanny as well as a maid who came and cleaned our house.

In my mind, servants did the dirty jobs—the menial tasks—that no one else wanted to do. No one would voluntarily choose to be a servant in India; you only did this if you had to. You were only a servant if it was the only option you had to make a living. In our house, we treated servants well enough, respected them, and did not abuse them, but largely we looked down on the servant class.

In India, there is a huge variation in how servants are treated. It all depends on whom you work for. Some find life very harsh and are forced to stay and work in horrible circumstances because they are in dire straits. The more desperate their need for income, the fewer choices available. Some have been sold into bonded labor; others have been trafficked and have no rights or way out. These servants are viewed as property and often treated worse than the owner's pets. They know they are replaceable and live under a cloud of fear and abuse that this reality creates. And still, they are better off than the masses of beggars who live in extreme poverty as outcasts with no prospects even to serve.

But if a servant has a kind and decent master, then they can expect fair treatment. If a servant is particularly trustworthy and competent, they may live in the household alongside the master's family for many years and be treated very well. But there is no real security there. There is no covenant. No contract. A servant is free to walk away from their master on a whim. A master is free to dismiss their servant without cause or warning. Even a small disagreement or misunderstanding can be enough for dismissal.

Perhaps this is tied to the Hindu culture of the caste system that was all around us, but we were Anglo-Indians, so we had a slightly different view. As Catholics, we gave to the poor out of duty and compassion, and fundamentally, we believed everyone could get to the Cross and there find the mercy of God (although in our congregation, most were middle class). But deep down in my subconscious, I felt higher than servants. I certainly knew I didn't want to be one. Growing up, if I didn't feel like studying, I often found my motivation for obtaining a good education by thinking, "One day, I will have servants working for me!"

God had to redefine servanthood for me.

And He did.

I had no idea that being a servant of God could look like Joshua, the great general who led the Israelites into the Promised Land. I read the account of how he fell down with his face to the earth and worshipped before the Commander of the Lord's Army and said, "What does my Lord say to His servant?"[2] This context of a servant confronted my understanding of servanthood and shined a light on its distortion. My view of servanthood needed to be dismantled and relearned.

Becoming a willing and faithful servant was an important part of my progression from outsider to insider to servant to daughter to bride. I needed to experience the joy and humility of being a servant first. I couldn't skip over this part, or the pride so interwoven into the fabric of my identity could not have been unraveled. And a bride of Christ cannot approach Him wearing a garment sewn with the threads of pride.

I needed to experience the joy and humility of being a servant first—I couldn't skip over this part.

I was not yet ready to live as a daughter of God. I first needed to learn how to serve Him without thought of profit or reward—a huge challenge for a woman motivated by what she could earn!

I began my servanthood journey by responding faithfully to any request God made. Every time I was obedient to His prompting, I took another step. I was learning the ways of His household—He the master, I His servant. His character and nature were being shown to me request by request. I was experiencing His goodness as I became His hands and feet to others. I did not yet see myself as one seated at the table, but I gladly participated in helping to prepare the table. I was not yet part of the discussion, but I had access to the conversation. But perhaps the most important lesson of this servant season was understanding and embracing that I could have only one master. I could not serve God and mammon—money. I could not serve God and myself—my own interests and desires. If I allowed multiple masters, then I was not a true servant of God.

God alone was my master.

He is a jealous God, and He will tolerate allegiance to no other.[3] I struggled with this for many years. I did my best to serve God AND reconcile being driven by my need to earn money—and lots of it. Only through God's lovingkindness would I grow to understand that all of me must belong to all of Him.

None of this process was quick or easy. Years went by as I took one step forward and two steps back. Earning my way was a tall, strong, immovable part of my belief system. At that point in my life, I had never heard of and did not yet have the vocabulary to describe what an "orphan spirit" was—but I had one! I had deeply embedded fears of being rejected, punished, or overlooked by God. I felt I had to prove myself—prove my value and my worth; take care of myself; look out for myself; provide for myself.

Even as I served God, I found that I wanted credit with Him for performing the service—proof that I had earned His favor or His trust. Just as I was driven to provide for myself financially because I didn't really believe anyone else would, this deeply held core belief wound itself around my relationship with God.

Paul demonstrated the kind of love Jesus has for His bride to me. I was so happy to be out of my house and married to Paul. It was amazing. I responded to Paul's kindness. His freedom to say, "I love you" and "You're beautiful" were like a tonic to a thirsty soul. We planned a three-week honeymoon. We went up into the Rockies so we could drive down the West Coast, meandering our way, staying in bed and breakfasts along the route, and taking in the sights at a leisurely, relaxed pace.

But I couldn't enjoy it. I was still so driven to perform and do things that I could not let myself take three weeks off for pure leisure. The joy of being present in the moment and the value of connecting deeply with Paul, alone and set apart from the world, escaped me.

I suggested, "Why don't we cut our honeymoon short? We can go back home, and I can use the time to move my stuff from my parent's home to yours. We can always take a short vacation during winter break to Mexico or somewhere."

We cut our summer trip short. We changed our flights and returned home. I moved my things into Paul's apartment, we opened our wedding gifts, and I started school. I went straight from being under my father's authority and wanting to please him to living under my husband's authority. I was driven by my need to earn his love and respect. So, even though I was working a part-time job at the bank and attending school, I also worked extra hard at home to ensure the house was clean, the laundry done, and the food cooked to his liking.

In November, Paul came home one night and said, "I think the Lord is doing something with me. I believe I need to sell my business and enroll in Bible School."

The wild excitement of adventure welled up inside me, mixed with questions about how all of this would unfold. Though the way ahead was filled with uncertainty, deep down, I knew it would all eventually work out.

Bethel was a Pentecostal church, and a great deal of emphasis was placed on what God was calling you to do or be. So, when Paul communicated that he felt God was calling him to sell his business and go to Bible school, I wanted to support him in that.

As a teenager, whenever I was asked questions like "What is your calling?" "Why did God create you?" or "What is your purpose?" I gave the intentional response, "... to fund ministries." And while that sounded spiritual and was met with approval, I had a selfish motive. It's true; I wanted to be a philanthropist because deep down, I knew that you had to be wealthy and have more than enough to fund ministries. You can't give what you don't have. I wanted to be rich.

The Christian thing for a rich person to do is share their wealth to expand the Kingdom of God. It is a noble calling, but my heart had another motivation.

When Paul told me he felt God calling him to Bible college and be a pastor, I felt like the Father was saying, "You want to fund ministries, right? Let's start with your own husband."

It seemed like the joke was on me.

I prayed, "God, Paul is going to be working for You, so that means we will have the best of things. We cannot be poor and work for You. We need the best schools for our children, we need to live in the best towns, and we need the ability to go out to nice places to eat and demonstrate Your blessing on our lives.

"I will make a covenant with You," I continued, "I will support Paul, and I will back him up 100% as long as You have my back and cover me, so if Paul makes a wrong decision or has a consequence, neither the children nor I will suffer for it."

It would have been easier for Paul to attend Bible College in Canada, but three people spoke to him about attending Zion Bible College in Rhode Island independently of one another. So, instead of taking that jaunt to Mexico we promised ourselves, we used my winter break to check out the school.

When we arrived, the college had no guest rooms available on campus. They put us up in a hotel, which was totally unexpected, and their generosity blew my mind. That weekend, doors of blessing and opportunity opened to us continuously, and we were overwhelmed by God's goodness demonstrated by the people we encountered on campus.

When we returned home, we decided to pray about it separately and hear what the Lord was saying to each of us. When we came back together, it was clear that He was inviting us to come and join Him in a new adventure.

We answered, "Yes."

I still had 21 credits left to complete my degree and knew I needed to finish where I was. Transferring was out of the question. I knew that leaving Canada without my degree would be a huge setback to my career goals. So, I went to visit the Dean. Miraculously, he granted me special permission to enroll in five in-person and two online courses to earn all 21 credits needed for graduation the next semester.

Even I had no idea how I was going to be able to do it. Paul and I were very involved at Bethel—Sunday mornings, Sunday nights, prayer on Wednesdays, youth on Fridays, and I still had my part-time job!

In January, I enrolled in seven classes and went to work. In February, we found out we were pregnant. I felt like I was sleep-walking and sleep-talking as the days and nights melted into each other. But even with all of what I took on, God's incredible grace and favor met me. He carried me through. I stayed healthy; I got good grades—I even made the Dean's list!

Paul applied for a student visa, and I would be dependent on his visa, which meant that neither of us could work in the United States while he was there studying. "God," I prayed, "should I stay in Canada? Should Paul go on alone so I can remain here to support us financially? What would You have us do?"

We thought it over and talked about it, and I found myself praying, "Lord, we are not going to separate. You blessed us with a child, which means You will take care of the child. It is Your problem, not ours. You told us to come, and we answered with our yes. We will keep our word and trust You to keep Yours."

And with that, our decision was firm. I took my last exam on Friday, May 14, and the next morning, we loaded up the trailer and drove to Rhode Island so Paul could begin a summer class that began on Monday.

"God, it is Your problem, not ours. We will keep our word and trust You to keep Yours."

I followed Paul in the Mazda minivan, crying my head off. I was five months pregnant. We had no jobs and would not be allowed to get jobs on Paul's student visa. We had no insurance. We had $13,000 USD to our name, and Paul's tuition was $5,000 per semester. Even living in the married dorms, I had no idea how we would survive.

Early in June, we went to open an account at Citizen's bank, located just behind the campus. While talking with the lady, our conversation led to my background in banking, and I applied for a job there. I had a series of interviews and received an offer letter in mid-September.

Wonderful, right?

Except I had no work visa. I was a guest in the United States, dependent on Paul's student visa.

Paul and I drove from Rhode Island to Vermont and crossed the border into Canada. Then we turned around and re-entered the United States. I went to the counter and, very matter of fact, made my application for a visa. In order to be allowed to work in the U.S., I showed the officer my degree in Actuarial Mathematics. I showed him my qualifications for a TN visa (a non-immigrant classification that permits a qualified Canadian citizen to seek temporary entry into the United States to engage in business activities at a professional level.)

Then I showed him the offer letter from the bank. I did everything I could to work my mathematics degree into the conversation to frame the offer to work in customer service.

You see, a TN visa is only granted if your profession qualifies under certain regulations.

I stood there in my homemade dress, eight months pregnant, pleading with kind Officer Beadle to approve my request and put that official stamp on my visa. He had smile lines around his blue eyes and a head of white hair that betrayed him as a grandpa. He grilled me for twenty minutes, asking question after question before finally asking, "Do you need this degree to do this job?"

I looked down for a brief moment and breathed a prayer, *"God, if You are going to provide through this door, then You will open it. If not, You will provide some other way."* I looked back up at Officer Beadle and answered truthfully, "No. Anybody can do this job; you don't need a degree."

Paul looked at me quizzically, "What did you just say?"

I looked at Officer Beadle with hope shining in my eyes. He looked at me for a long moment, then he took out a stamp, stamped my visa, and said, "Welcome to the United States. Congratulations on your new job!"

We drove back to Rhode Island, and Monday morning, I reported to the bank for orientation. As I began filling out my paperwork, I told them, "Okay, I have my offer letter, and I have my visa. I'll run down to the Social Security office at lunchtime and get my number, then finish these forms in the afternoon. Okay?"

I had no idea this was not normal. I had no clue that this wasn't the way things usually worked. But at noon, I went downtown, waddled into the SSA lobby, and went to the counter. There was no one there.

"Excuse me," I called out. "Hello, is there someone here who can help me?"

A middle-aged woman appeared, and I explained my situation and how I needed my social security number that afternoon.

Without further inquiry, she said, "Okay," and I left with a social security number and a temporary card until an official one came in the mail.

No one told me this was not how the government worked. No one informed me that this was impossible and would take a miracle. I walked into the border office and the Social Security Administration expecting the mountains to move—and they did!

Our son, Joshua, was born just a few weeks after I began my job, and I left for three months on maternity leave. I returned in February to work in customer service at the Citizens Bank in Woonsocket, Rhode Island, one of the poorest towns. On the first and third of every month, a line of people formed, waiting for their Social Security and Disability checks. Walking downtown, I encountered teens with no teeth from taking drugs. Everywhere there were teens with prams pushing their children. I wondered, *God, how are we going to prosper here?*

I knew working hard was my part, so I made sure I worked hard enough to make enough money so Paul wouldn't have to worry about our finances. I could not grasp that I had nothing to prove, nothing to hide, and nothing to lose in God.

I was the first to arrive at the office and the last to leave. If someone needed help in another branch, I volunteered to fill in. I was driven by earning money and did whatever it took to be successful, even when that meant working 60-70 hours a week. Rebekah was born, and Paul continued to study hard and care for the children. He shuttled them back and forth to daycare—the fees for this were higher than his tuition! He fed them and got them dressed. I didn't even know their doctor's names!

I justified my dedication to my job, rationalizing, "If I do this, then Paul doesn't have to be concerned about finances. He won't have to worry about where the money will come from. After all, he is on a student visa and is not permitted to work. He can take care of the kids and focus on school. I'll earn the money. This is so Paul can minister and fulfill his calling." I was too busy working to get to the top.

And I did get to the top. My career soared.

In that poor town, the Lord prospered me. I brought in so much business that I was awarded Top Banker, and we won a trip to Aruba—making up for the trip to Mexico we never got to take. I had favor at the bank, favor with clients, and everything I put my hands to prospered.

I was a very good salesperson. My early McDonald's training informed me that if I served people well, I would win their trust and make the sale. I knew if I listened to them and gave them what they needed or wanted, I would end up with the best sales numbers. Serving clients was my ticket to top performance. I had no trouble being *this* kind of servant.

I knew I needed God's favor, God's provision, and protection, but I viewed it more like a contract than a covenant.

I knew the Lord was at the back of all that, providing and opening doors of opportunity, but I also knew that I was driving our success by working so hard. I knew I needed God's favor, God's provision, and protection, but I viewed it more like a contract than a covenant.

"God, I'll do this part really well; then You will do that part." I had no intimacy in my relationship with Him. My prayers were laundry lists of requests and thank-you notes for answers.

Whenever I achieved a goal, I immediately set a new one. Money is an exacting master. It demands more from you than it provides for you. You must work more and more and more. Harder and harder. There is never enough. What you did last quarter must be topped this quarter. The more of it I made, the more it demanded from me to earn.

Meanwhile, Paul graduated and began working as a pastor. Eventually, he became the executive pastor of Celebration International Church. By this time, I was very well established in mortgage banking, and I had a big head about it. But I knew how to play the game. I knew the right words to say, and I was determined to be supportive of Paul. I went to church twice on Sunday and every Wednesday night. I backed up all his decisions, and the church grew.

I was never willing to embrace the label "pastor's wife." My career was too important to me. Paul was the pastor, and I had my own career. I would never be one of those pastor's wives who knew how to sing and play the piano. I didn't want to teach Sunday School or help out in the nursery. I had no desire to preach or counsel, or visit the sick. I didn't know the references of where things were in the Bible. I dutifully attended all the required meetings, but I was not really involved. I viewed my role of serving Paul by making a good living as my service to God, so Paul was free to minister. I was fine with the added byline to my spiritual resume as "the wife of a pastor." I was proud of Paul and wanted to serve God—I just didn't want any of that to interfere with my *real* career.

It's true; I no longer felt like an outsider. And now, I was even more than an insider. I was a valued member of the team—I was a servant in the Kingdom. I just did it from that orphan mentality. I had not yet grasped what it meant to be God's child. An heir. A joint heir with Jesus. Providing excellent service was my ticket to success in my career. So, I was really good with providing excellent service in the Kingdom. It wasn't truly a heart thing yet—it was still an exchange for value.

Mortgage banking experienced a refinancing boom in 2008, and I was determined to "make hay while the sun shines." Another bank poached me, paying a lot of money to get me. The sun shone brightly month after month, well into 2013. I worked long days, 14-16 hours, originating and closing loans. I earned BIG money and kept telling myself, "You have made it!" I was living my definition of success: I could buy anything I desired without having to look at the price tag—and that felt amazing.

Of course, I had neither the time nor the energy to go shopping and spend any of that money I was piling up.

I sat one afternoon in a board room full of high-powered executive men and three Caucasian women. I was the youngest and a minority. I felt validated, and I was at the pinnacle of my career. I attended a bank event in San Francisco, and Paul and the kids went along to visit Yosemite Park. They picked me up after the conference, and we went to visit Paul's cousin before going to the airport for our flight home.

While Paul drove, I discovered I could not feel my right arm. It was limp and dead. I couldn't speak properly. Somehow, I managed to communicate that something was wrong, and we stopped at a pharmacy for aspirin. The numbness went away, but my speech was slow. We ate dinner, and I stayed close to Paul. My mind was clear, but I had trouble speaking. If someone asked me a question, I looked at Paul, and he would answer for me.

We boarded a Red Eye back to Boston, and the next day I returned to work, but I knew something was wrong. I struggled through a call with a client, then telephoned my sister. My speech was muddled, and she said, "Get yourself to a hospital—now!"

I was admitted, but they could not figure out exactly what had happened. I had a TIA, then three days later, they told me they found a hole in my heart. They tried to put me on medication for cholesterol, gave me a shot in my belly, and ran tests ... all the things doctors do for patients. I was most concerned about my speech. I was still talking much more slowly than usual, so they offered speech therapy, but recommended that if I threw myself back into work and talked as much as I could, it would all come back.

That suited me fine. Throwing myself into my work was what I did best! But I was concerned. I had just been brought over to this new position with a large salary increase, and now my production was off. My performance suffered, but I clawed my way back through long hours and hard work.

Of course, I was still the "wife of a pastor," but I was living two lives. I served two masters. I set no limits or boundaries on how much I worked daily. I rarely attended anything "extra" from the church. I popped in and out of church meetings, taking calls and answering emails, closing loans, and feeling very important. Jackie Doucette, an associate pastor at the church, invited me to attend a women's retreat for ministers and pastors' wives. I'm not sure why, but I didn't give my default answer, "Oh, I'm sorry, I would love to go, but I am just far too busy to attend." Maybe I just wanted to be included. Perhaps I didn't want to feel left out. Whatever the reason, I stepped out of character and said, "Yes, I would love to join you!"

It was terrible timing. I had a mountain of work I needed to complete, and I arrived not having any idea why I had agreed to go. But one of the speakers spoke a word that pierced my soul. Her message affected me deeply and laid the groundwork for the Holy Spirit to begin pruning, purging, and purifying my heart and renewing my mind.

When I came home, I heard Holy Spirit say, "I want you to stop all secular entertainment. No more television shows for the next year."

What? I wondered. This seemed an impossible task. I worked such long hours and had such intense, stressful days, that when I came home, I loved binging shows on Netflix to help me power down and unwind. I liked *NCIS*, *Nikita*, and *Alias*. They relaxed me. They were my coping mechanism. *Why would God ask me to give that up?*

But the words spoken at the retreat had softened the ground of my heart. I was growing hungry for something deeper than Master/servant. I wanted to *know* Him. Holy Spirit is in the business of making the impossible possible, so I said, "I would love to do it. I want to do it, but I cannot do it unless You help me." I knew I needed His grace to let go of this crutch. I was learning to serve Him for the joy of service, not for a reward. So, when I came home from long days now, I picked up a book instead and began reading.

> I was hungry for something deeper than Master/servant. I wanted to *know* Him.

I started with *The Circle Maker* by Mark Batterson—a book I had noticed on my sister Roshni's side table. Slowly, my thought life changed. My prayer life changed. My mind was being renewed bit by bit. I read my Bible more and devoured books that taught me to know God and love Him deeply. As I swam in and drank from different sources of living water, the world's dirt slowly began to wash away. I listened to sermons from Robert Morris, Bill Johnson, David Hogan, Dan Mohler, and Myles Munroe. One of Dr. Monroe's teachings about fasting went right through my soul like a two-edged sword. He said, "You don't even know your God on an empty belly." Those ten words turned my life upside down. I started with a three-day water fast. Then seven. Then twenty-one. Eventually, and only by His grace, I fasted for forty days.

Each time my Master, Jesus, asked me to fast and I answered yes, He showed me new dimensions of Himself. I completed the whole year without secular entertainment—and I was forever changed.

My eyes were opened to so many things now. I was learning to embrace God in a richer, fuller way. I served Him out of love—even adventure. I was back in good health and joked, "I'm *never* leaving this job unless I get fired. I will retire from here." And I was almost back on top at the office ... until ...

... I got laid off.

Forty-five people were let go. *Who lays off Yvonne Allen?* I thought indignantly. *I don't even get paid unless I produce!* I did my best to keep a straight face, fighting back the tears. I went back to my office and called Paul. I was given from noon until 5:00 PM to wrap everything up, transition my clients, send out any final emails, and pack my things.

I went home hollow. *Tomorrow, I have no job. I have nothing. I have no emails to answer. No calls to make or return. Who am I? What am I called to do?* I was in turmoil.

I recalled David Hogan sharing how when he came to the end of his understanding and needed answers from the Lord, he would let his wife know, go into his office, shut the door, and not come out until God answered him.

That's what I'm gonna do, I thought. I talked it over with Paul and the kids. Joshua was 13, and Rebekah was 11, and this would be the first time they ever had me without a phone in my hand and a dozen emails on my mind, so I didn't want to just disappear without the family being on board. I think they all sensed how lost and small I felt and gave me their full support.

I had turned a guest room into a closet some time ago—I needed it for my growing inventory of work clothes and dress shoes. I decided I would make that my prayer closet and not come out until I had answers from the Lord.

I was already baptized, but the year seeking God had changed me. I embraced the work of sanctification, and I desired to be baptized again before I entered my closet. Paul baptized me on Sunday, July 6, 2014, at Wayland Township beach.

It was time to enter the closet.

While sequestered, God spoke to me that I needed to discard and burn all the old letters, poems, and cards from relationships with old boyfriends. I had saved and cherished these for a long time. Immediately, I responded by putting them all in a paper bag, and early the next morning, before anyone was up, I started to burn them in the backyard firepit.

I was a city girl. I didn't know you couldn't just chuck a whole bag of cards and papers on the fire and expect them to light up. That pile of history was not ready to go so easily. I had to retrieve the bag and place them in the fire just a few at a time, sometimes one at a time.

It was a process. It was a cleansing, healing, restorative process. I had to keep the fire stoked and hot to complete the work. As my old life turned to ash, I was reborn. God had long since forgiven all my sins. Now I was learning to forgive myself and let all the baggage go.

God showed me that I had clung to my career as an idol. It was a monument to self-sufficiency. He reminded me of my cavalier, "I will never leave this job unless I get fired," and that I had to be let go in order to come out of that place and enter the land He had prepared for me.

Dying to self is not for the weak or faint of heart.

Now that I had burned the records of my past, Holy Spirit confronted me about one more skeleton in my closet. His kindness is so complete that He leaves no ammunition for the enemy, so in my place of surrender, He whispered to me, *"Pay them back."*

My heart sank. Though I had not thought about this in years, I knew exactly who He was talking about and what He meant—my Aunty Mina and Uncle Larry. My first response was to reason my way out of it. "Lord, I already asked YOU for forgiveness. You have wiped my slate clean."

"Yes, I have. Your slate with *Me* is clean. I am inviting you to humble yourself and ask *them* for forgiveness."

The next time I was in Toronto for a family event, I sought out a moment alone with Aunty Mina and Uncle Larry. It came when I rode back with them from a family member's baptism at mass. I had the money to repay them in my pocket, and I was glad to do it. Relieved. But bringing myself to tell them I had stolen from them all those years ago—twenty-three years earlier—was incredibly hard. My pulse raced, and my mouth felt dry. These people had trusted me. Loved me. Helped my family migrate from India to Canada, employing us while we got on our feet. *How could I tell them I stole from them?*

The enemy whispered arguments to cover it up, "Just say the money is a gift—why hurt them?"

So, before I let that argument soak in, I blurted out, "I need to tell you something," then I confessed my teenage trespasses to them and how Holy Spirit had convicted me, and handed the money back.

"Oh, sweetie," Aunty Mina said, "that's okay; there is no need to pay us back."

Uncle Larry grabbed the money playfully and began counting it out loud, laughing as he said, "Thank you very much!"

It was humbling and liberating at the same time.

Surrendering the identity that you have built to embrace the one God has created for you can only be done as He enables you with His great grace. Jesus said, "If anyone desires to come after Me, let him deny himself, and take up his cross daily, and follow Me." [4]

Pride had to go.

Sin had to go.

Excuses had to go.

Apart from God, I can do nothing. I must remain in Him as He remains in me so I can bear fruit. [5]

At last, I was beginning to truly grasp the beauty of being a servant. "The Son of Man did not come to be served, but to serve, and to give His life a ransom for many" [6]—for me! God knows me by name. He has called me to serve Him.

> *Listen to me, all you in distant lands!*
> *Pay attention, you who are far away!*
> *The Lord called me before my birth; from*
> *within the womb, He called me by name.*
> *He made my words of judgment as sharp as a sword.*

SERVANT

He has hidden me in the shadow of His hand.
I am like a sharp arrow in His quiver.

He said to me, "You are my servant,
Israel, and you will bring me glory."

I replied, "But my work seems so useless!
I have spent my strength for nothing
and to no purpose.
Yet I leave it all in the Lord's hand;
I will trust God for my reward."

And now the Lord speaks—
the one who formed me in my mother's
womb to be His servant, who commissioned
me to bring Israel back to Him.
The Lord has honored me, and my
God has given me strength.

He says, "You will do more than restore
the people of Israel to me.
I will make you a light to the Gentiles, and you
will bring my salvation to the ends of the earth."

The Lord, the Redeemer and Holy One of Israel,
says to the one who is despised and rejected by the
nations, to the one who is the servant of rulers:
"Kings will stand at attention when you pass by.
Princes will also bow low because of
the Lord, the faithful one, the Holy One
of Israel, who has chosen you."[7]

When I first began to serve the Lord, I tried to obey and do what He told me to do. I was busy learning how He liked things done—His likes and dislikes, His expectations. I wanted to make sure I did things according to the rules.

As I progressed, I began to know Him better. I could anticipate His requests before He made them. I began to learn how things functioned in His household. I began to better understand the way my Master thought, and I could serve Him from a glad heart and not wait to be told what to do.

Eventually, as my identity became clearer, I began to understand that I could speak on His behalf, with His authority. I am His emissary. His ambassador. His trusted general. My loyalty is sure, and my desire to honor Him and serve the Kingdom was no longer in question.

I had one Master. He alone would I serve.

And as I yielded to this new dimension of servanthood, God invited me to go deeper with Him still. He did not want me to remain in the station of servant to the House; He wanted to call me friend.

ENDNOTES

1.   Song of Songs 2:11, TPT.

2.   Joshua 5:14b, NIV.

3.   See Exodus 34:14.

4.   Luke 9:23, NKJV.

5.   See John 15:8.

6.   Matthew 20:28, NIV.

7.   Isaiah 49:1-7, NLT.

Friend

Chapter Five

FRIEND

... and left it bright with blossoming flowers.
The season for singing and pruning
the vines has arrived.
I hear the cooing of doves in our land,
filling the air with songs
to awaken you and guide you forth.[1]

THE BRIDEGROOM KING

A popular person never seems at a loss for friends. While it is true that popularity sees no shortage of fair-weather companions, it does not equate to enduring friendships or faithful confidants. In Mumbai, I was popular, but I had only a few close friends—a mere handful. Our family's migration to Canada left me starting over again, and there I buried myself in school and work and earning money. I didn't have time to foster deep or meaningful connections.

By twenty-three, I was married to Paul and living in Rhode Island, working hard to help support the family while Paul focused on his studies at Zion Bible College. It was another fresh start. Another new place. Another set of people to befriend, but to me, these were really more acquaintances. I didn't feel I had the time to develop lasting friendships.

Next up—Boston. Here we settled for several years. Paul was very involved in the ministry, and of course, I supported him and was involved at a level appropriate as the wife of a pastor, but my biggest time investment was in my career. I was *really* good at my job. There, I was confident. Important. Valuable. And I liked earning money. I liked it a little too much. I had many casual friendships, but other than Paul; I had never really experienced what a deep friendship might be.

When I turned thirty-eight, we moved again, this time to the Dallas/Fort Worth Metroplex. I surveyed the long list of contacts on my phone. I knew many, many people. But how many of them was I close to? As time and distance eroded the opportunities for interaction, I soon learned how superficial many of my connections had been. Circumstantial. When the season of shared life experience ended, the friendships waned.

When we got to Dallas, I wasn't sure if I had any real confidants— you know, the kind you can call at 3:00 am, the kind with whom you can share your deepest secrets without fear of judgment, the kind who encourage you, tell you what you need to hear (not what you want to hear), and who will push you to become everything God has called you to be.

I had a real deficit here. I had not been that kind of friend, and I did not have those kinds of friends. I wasn't even certain how to go about changing the situation. But that's right about the time when Holy Spirit turned my world upside down, put His finger right in the middle of my career, and demonstrated that friendship with Him was the absolute greatest and most wonderful friendship of all.

One day, I sat with my Bible and read, "I no longer call you servants because a servant does not know His master's business. Instead, I have called you friends, for everything that I learned from My Father I have made known to you."[2]

I paused and reread the line, "I have called you **friends** ..."

Friends, I pondered. When He said these stunning words, Jesus was talking to His disciples here, not long before His journey to the Cross. He took these men—His *friends*—with Him to the Garden of Gethsemane, where He agonized and wrestled with the path destiny had set before Him. He did not hide this grief from His disciples—He invited them to tarry with Him in the middle of it. His guard was lowered. He wore no mask. Jesus shared not only His thoughts and feelings with them but also the thoughts of God, the Father. He brought them—His *friends*—into His purpose. He held nothing back.

I could not think of a truer definition of friendship than this. It reveals that friendship with Jesus involves the deepest level of trust. The most intimate exchange of thought. The truest revelation of motives. The most unmasked, unfiltered access to the heart. Coming to the Triune God—Father, Son, and Holy Spirit—as a *friend* is no trivial or superficial matter. Our connection to Them is not circumstantial or convenient. Friendship with God lays everything bare.

Until now, I had come to God as it aligned with the pursuit of my own interests. I prayed for safety for my family and fulfillment for my children. I asked for provision, for open doors, and opportunities. I thanked God for my daily bread. I thanked Him for His blessings.

I came to Him in crisis. I read His Word from duty or when I had a topic to study. But at the core, I pursued God for positive outcomes. I did not yet comprehend that God pursued me for a relationship. I had no idea what it meant to be His friend. I had only just become comfortable thinking of myself as His loyal, loving, and faithful servant.

Now God was telling me I was no longer (just) His servant; He called me His **friend**. He was lovingly, tenderly, patiently inviting me to explore a new level of relationship with Him.

My journey with the Lord had developed to the place where I desired to embrace whatever He had for me—even if I didn't understand it or know how to appropriate it. If God was inviting me into intimate friendship with Him, then I wanted to answer His invitation.

I decided to fast for forty days to seek His face. Shortly before I began, I heard an evangelist say, "When you start a fast, you should have a list of prayer points." That sounded like sound advice. He had recommended that you have about ten, so I made a list of fifteen. (I am, after all, a super achiever!) These included things like having more faith, taking away any unbelief, having the gift of healing, and so on ... all very spiritual things—religious things. Altruistic, in my opinion. So, I felt I was off to a good start.

I took my list and dutifully looked up scripture to match each one, just to be certain my prayer points were all holy and sanctioned. I wanted to get this friend-with-God thing off to a good start! Armed with my list, I nobly began my forty-day fast.

On day twenty-one, I set off for my favorite booth at Central Market Café. This was my regular habit now, and I genuinely looked forward to meeting with Holy Spirit at "our" favorite corner booth. It was a regular morning. Unremarkable. It was sunny and clear, and all the regulars were there at their regular tables having their regular meals. I was fasting, of course, so no food for me. Just my Bible and my journal ... and, of course, my list.

Instrumental music played in the background, just like it did every day. I surveyed the room, marveling at how peaceful and quiet it was for me, even with the activity of people coming and going and chatting and eating. As always, I sat facing the chair I reserved for Him, and we talked. I glanced down at my list, trying to decide which point to talk with Him about today; I even paused dramatically, waiting to see if He would prompt me about which one.

But He did something different.

Gently but firmly, as only a trusted friend would do, He said, "Yvonne, why have you come to Me with a list? Do you go meet your other friends with lists?"

My jaw dropped. Something in my stomach did a little flip as realization began to dawn.

"If a friend kept showing up at your house," He continued, "and each time brought you a list of things for you to do or to talk about, you would soon decide you didn't really want to be friends with them anymore."

I nodded, "You're right," I whispered; the list in front of me felt like a glowing neon sign, drawing unwanted attention.

"What would you think if every time your friends came to visit you, they always asked you for something? If they only ever came around for what you could do for them or give to them, you would see them as moochers—not as true friends, wouldn't you?"

I was stunned.

> ## Conviction flooded my soul as my perception of friendship forever changed.

I was completely taken off guard. Conviction flooded my soul as my perception of friendship forever changed. In an instant, I understood. Tears brimmed in my eyes as I thought of how I had hurt Him; what an insult it was to presume my coming to Him with a list was the act of a devoted, loving friend.

"I'm sorry," I breathed. I'm not sure if I said the words out loud or not, because time stood still. I didn't hear the music or the diners or the clinking of flatware against plates. All I heard was the sound of my heart beating, and all I felt was the desire to rush into His arms and bury my face in His neck. I was undone.

"I want to be **friends**," He said.

"I want to be **your** friend."

I wiped my tears. Little droplets had fallen and blurred the ink on my offending list. I tore the list from my journal, crumpled it, and let His words sink deeply into my heart.

"I want **you** to be **_My_ friend**," He finished, and the tears rolled down my face unchecked.

Something inside me had changed. Forever changed. I caught the spirit of friendship and marveled at the gift He had just offered me. _Friendship with God!_

"If You don't ever answer another prayer," I whispered, "I am fine," and I meant it. "You have done SO much for me already—our friendship, my devotion—does not depend on You doing things for me. I know it is okay for me to ask You for things, but now I understand that isn't the point of our friendship. You are not my Sugar Daddy, and

I am not a mooch. We are friends. We break bread together. Share life together. Swap stories. Laugh. Cry. Sit in silence. We spend time together for the joy of fellowship, not for the purpose of industry."

I looked at the crumpled list in my hand. I wished I had an altar where I could burn it and offer it as a sacrifice right there. God was my friend!

I knew He loved me, no matter what. I knew He could show up in good times when I had made preparation to meet with Him and gone to some effort because I loved Him and anticipated with joy our time together. I also knew He could show up in the worst times when I was unlovely and unlovable. I didn't need to prepare or pretend. His love for me was unconditional. It was true.

I was just beginning to grasp the very surface of what that kind of love meant.

- **I had no need to prove my love for Him.**

  This sounds like a simple sentence, and perhaps you nodded your head in easy agreement. But this was a HUGE shift in my approach to God. My whole life had been built on saying and doing the right things in order to be acceptable. Doing nothing to receive love was as foreign to me as living at the bottom of the ocean.

- **There were no boxes to check off to demonstrate my discipline or devotion.**

  This concept flew in the face of my Indian heritage. It shook to the core my Catholic upbringing. Everything about both had taught me that duty was godliness. Following the rules and doing the right things was all that had ever been expected of me.

- **Whatever I said or did—it did not change His love for me!**

  How could that be? I marveled. God's love for me was unquestioned. Unchallenged. Unconditional.

The really astonishing thing to me was how well He knew me. How He spoke my language—not just the one I talked in and used to write letters, but He spoke the language of my heart, the language of my soul. He knew me intimately and discerned just what I would respond to and why. He met me right where I was, exactly when I was ready to receive this revelation and not one minute before.

Perfect love. Before-the-foundation-of-the-world-I-knew-you love.

That love transformed my heart.

Fellowship with God is fellowship with light. He is light. In Him, there is no darkness at all.[3] As we draw closer to Him, we draw closer to the light. That light is full of love and warmth, as pleasurable as sitting on the beach beside the ocean on a bright, clear day.

That light is also like a beacon, shining brightly and safely guiding us into a safe harbor if we are lost and caught up in the storms of life.

But that light is also as exacting and magnifying as a surgeon's lamp, revealing our sin and not shrinking from our dysfunction or chaos or masking our ugliest parts. This light reveals—all of you. And the revelation is without shame. The exposure has a divine purpose. It is completely bathed in love, illuminating all that is in us that must be yielded to Him so we can receive the full measure of His grace and remove all that separates us from knowing His great love.

It is uncomfortable.

Challenging.

We are tempted to flee. To cover ourselves, as Adam and Eve did in the Garden. The unwavering light of God can only be endured by those who surrender their hearts willingly and completely and invite His presence to purify and cleanse. There is nothing to hide. We must surrender all.

One evening, I heard Pastor Tim Ross share a message on "Face to Face Encounters," where he said, "We need to start giving our unedited testimonies," this caught my attention. "The church would be so much more powerful if we did not care how we were looked at by people, but only that God is glorified," he continued.

The message made a powerful impression on me. Later, as I thought about it, I realized that what Moses shared in his final words in the book of Deuteronomy was what Pastor Tim meant by an "unedited testimony." Moses included all the unimpressive (and somewhat embarrassing) details about the wilderness journey. He wasn't trying to impress anyone; he was just faithfully recording God's faithfulness to an unfaithful people.

Could I do that? Would I?

The root of pride was deep in my life. Fear of man and fear of what others thought of me had long been a motivator for many of my choices. I was image conscious. I felt the light of God shining on this pride, revealing this fear, and this time, instead of covering it up, I invited Him in. I welcomed the exposure, as a cancer patient welcomes the surgeon's skill.

"Have your way, Lord," I prayed. "I offer my pride into Your care. I release my fear. I grant You full access."

Immediately, I knew what He was asking of me.

That weekend, I was supposed to speak to a group of believers in Montreal, Canada. With pride under my feet, I knew I had to share my own "unedited testimony" of something that had happened a while back. I needed to demonstrate the faithfulness of God even when I was not. Here is what I shared:

I began working for a new firm at the height of my career. One of the associates took me under his wing, trying, I thought, to be my friend and business partner. We went on calls to see clients together, handled mutual customers, and he gave me many opportunities. It was all very subtle.

Because we worked together so closely, we naturally shared a camaraderie. We grew very comfortable around each other, in and out of each other's offices, sharing lunches, and talking business—and life. Before long, I was answering his emails and texts after hours. If he texted me at 8:00 pm, I texted back. We laughed at each other's jokes, and he understood the world where I obtained so much affirmation.

Before I realized it, I was having an emotional affair with this man. We never did anything inappropriate, or that crossed the line as most people would measure it, but in my heart, I knew I was granting him access to parts of my soul that should be reserved for Paul alone. Holy Spirit spoke to me, and the words of Proverbs rang true, "The wise woman builds her house, but with her own hands, the foolish one tears hers down."[4]

I knew it was true. I had a good marriage to a man who never did anything but love me, show me respect, and offer me his loyalty and affection. I had a great family and an awesome job. *What am I doing?* I wondered. I had been so blinded; I didn't see how this relationship had slowly turned into a violation of Paul's trust. It had begun so harmlessly. Just business. "There's a way that seems right to a man," I heard, "but in the end, it leads to death."[5]

Holy Spirit's conviction brought me to repentance. I confessed my sin and received God's forgiveness. But I knew I also needed to confess to Paul. "Even if I stop texting him right now," I said, "I don't want this to be a skeleton in my closet." Dread flooded me.

That evening, I sat on the bed as Paul came in. "I need to tell you something," I said, my voice wavered. My mouth was dry. I couldn't look at him; I was so ashamed. Paul sat down on the bed beside me, waiting.

I felt the heat from his body, and I felt like pulling away. This man had only ever loved me. He had literally been Jesus to me. *Even saying this to him will hurt him,* I thought. I couldn't bring myself to speak. I was crying, staring at the floor.

"What is it, darling," He asked tenderly. "Whatever it is, it's okay. You can tell me anything."

And I knew he meant it.

If I don't do it now, I never will, I thought, *and I need to do it.* Shame engulfed me. I felt small and filthy. Through my tears and sorrow, I confessed it all to Paul. I held nothing back. He sat in stillness, listening patiently, not interrupting, asking no questions. Finally, after a pause, I said, "and I have now broken off all ties. I no longer respond to his texts. In fact, I have blocked him on my phone, and I avoid him at work as much as possible."

I could feel Paul's gaze, but I couldn't bring myself to meet it. My cheeks were flushed with shame. He took his hand and lifted my chin until my eyes met his. There was no anger. There was no confusion on his face, no questioning. If he was hurt or felt betrayed, he did not show it. He said only, "I love you. You are a good wife. You are beautiful ..." and at that, I pulled my face away and lowered my eyes again. I would have preferred him to be angry with me. I deserved his anger.

"No," he lifted my chin again. "Don't you understand? You are a good woman. A beautiful woman, and I love you with all my heart."

He engulfed me in an embrace as I cried bitter tears, unable to fathom how I could have behaved this way when I had such a man loving me in this way.

In the end, Paul was not mad. He never yelled at me. He

forgave me right there. He never brought it up again. He never checked my phone or my computer. He is so secure in who he is and in his love for me that he has never once—not ever—even mentioned it again.

Paul's response to me was such a picture of Jesus. For the first time, I could fathom what the Psalmist meant when he said, "As far as the east is from the west, so far has he removed our transgressions from us."[6] Paul covered my sin with his love. Paul covered my nature with his. Paul fulfilled the marriage covenant with his vow.

In this, Paul demonstrated to me what true forgiveness looks like. He showed me what a true friend is. He exacted no penalty, demanded no explanation or penance, he didn't even ask me to earn back his trust. He covered me completely in his love, and his favor and affection for me never wavered in the slightest.

Through shameless tears, I shared my full, unedited testimony with this Montreal church, dealing a death blow to my pride.

God was glorified.

The more I drew near to God, the more God drew near to me, just like He promised in His Word.[7] He was showing me how to be friends—more specifically, how to be His friend. He spoke to me through everyday circumstances and through everyday people who had no idea He was using them to speak life into me.

One incident stood out to me as I transitioned from servant to friend. I was in the interview process, looking to secure a position as a loan officer. A few different mortgage companies were courting me. They would fly me in from Boston, take me to the best restaurants, and give me the red-carpet treatment in their attempts to reel me in. It was gratifying.

One company was Embrace Home Loans, and their CEO and President, Dennis Hardiman, made the pitch. He likely did not know that Holy Spirit was flowing through him to demonstrate something to me when he reached out to schedule another meeting. But I knew I would not accept their offer, so I told Dennis, "I don't want you spending any more time or resources on me."

"Yvonne," Dennis exclaimed, "you are worth it! You are worth it today, you are worth it tomorrow, and you will be worth it a year from now!"

It was Dennis speaking the words, but the message was from God—I was worth it. I was worth it today. I was worth it tomorrow. I was worth it for eternity.

My heart soared!

Another benefit of being God's friend is that He seems to really enjoy introducing you around to His friends! It is such a joy to be loved by God through the lives and obedience of others around you.

God enjoys introducing you to His friends!

Sometimes, I get busy. My calendar fills up, and I can get focused on the daily routine and get wrapped up in my details. Even though I am very careful not to bring God a list anymore, sometimes I can still just go about my business ticking off things I want or need, chattering away without ever stopping to hear Him speak.

God likes talking to me. And when I give Him room, I have found that He can be very talkative—even funny. He has so much to tell me! When I remember to zip up, stay quiet, and listen to Him, He never fails to communicate. Of course, I love the deep revelation and meaningful conversations we have, but I have also come to really love and appreciate His humor. Sometimes He is absolutely hilarious!

One Wednesday morning, I said to Him, "You haven't been funny lately," and I went about my business, preparing the house for a Bible study we were hosting on Thursday. Typically, we have about forty-five people gather weekly to worship the Lord and study His Word together. As I straightened and cleaned later that evening, I told Paul, "We don't have enough toilet paper in the house for tomorrow; we need to get some more."

"No, no, we have enough. You don't need to worry about it," he replied.

I knew there were a lot of kids attending with their parents—and kids can really go through a *lot* of toilet paper, so I insisted again, "Paul, I mean it. We don't have enough toilet paper!"

Paul smiled at me and said, "If you can find at least eight rolls of toilet paper in this house, then there is absolutely no need to go to the store and buy more. We have enough."

So, we ran around to all five bathrooms, checking under the cabinets to count rolls, and I really wanted to cheat to prove him wrong and say we didn't have enough—but I was honest. I came out triumphantly and told Paul, "Well, we have only seven rolls, so ..."

We went to the store and bought more toilet paper.

The next day as people began to gather for Bible study, a young girl who had never before been to our home came to the door carrying a huge package of toilet paper! As I answered the doorbell, she said, "Don't look at me funny, but when I was driving to your house, I passed the Tom Thumb and heard Holy Spirit say, 'Stop and buy toilet paper.' I just sat there thinking it was so weird—I mean, don't people usually show up with cookies or water or flowers or something? Who brings toilet paper to a Bible study? I felt ridiculous, so I came all the way here. But when I tried to get out of the car, I heard Holy Spirit say, 'Go back and buy toilet paper.' So, I did."

There she was, carrying a family pack of nine rolls. I couldn't believe it! I started laughing, and I shared the story of how I had teased God about not being funny lately—so He sent me toilet paper from a stranger (now a friend) to prove His sense of humor was intact!

He is God in the details, and just as a good friend does, He shows up in the most lovely and unexpected ways.

He cares about our lives. He enjoys being a part of your day—and not just in the big life-changing decisions, but in the everyday stuff that makes living worthwhile. He is God in the details, and just as a good friend does, He shows up in the most lovely and unexpected ways.

It is no longer a discipline to carve out daily time to spend with God. My soul longs for these moments. I need them like I need air and water. He draws me to His side, and willingly I answer His call. I want time with Him—quality time where He is the center of my focus, and I am the apple of His eye. The Psalmist's words whisper to my heart:

"Come and talk with Me."

... and my heart responds, "Lord, I am coming ...

Teach me how to live, O Lord.

Lead me along the right path ...

Yet I am confident I will see the Lord's goodness while I am

here in the land of the living.

Wait patiently for the Lord.

Be brave and courageous.

Yes, wait patiently for the Lord."[8]

Bill Johnson[9] says, "Absolute surrender to the will of God is the only way for the believer to live. Yet something strange happens as that person enters into the intimacy of friendship with God; God becomes interested in our desires. And ultimately, He wants our minds renewed so that our will can be done."

I have found this to be true. The more I draw near to God, the more my nature yields to His. The more time I spend in His presence, the more my desires align with His. The more surrendered my heart becomes, the more I partake of His Spirit, and the more my will gets lost—becomes engulfed in His. There is less and less separation because I am more and more consumed by Him. My will begins to take on the shape of His will. The image of God in me gets sharper and clearer. Paul said it this way:

Beloved friends, what should be our proper response to
God's marvelous mercies? I encourage you to surrender
yourselves to God to be His sacred, living sacrifices.

And live in holiness, experiencing all that delights His heart.

For this becomes your genuine expression of worship.

Stop imitating the ideals and opinions of the culture around you, but be inwardly transformed by the Holy Spirit through a total reformation of how you think.

This will empower you to discern God's will as you live a beautiful life, satisfying and perfect in His eyes."[10]

Jim Rohn[11] says, "Show me the five people you spend the most time with, and I will show you your future." Many leadership experts hold this to be true. We become like those we hang around. You pick up their speech patterns, begin thinking alike, and take on their habits and characteristics. If true, wouldn't you want three of these five friends to be the Father, Son, and Holy Spirit?

The more time I spend with Them, the more I think, speak, and act as They would.

God had taken me from outsider to insider to servant, and now He continued to draw me in to experience Him in this new dimension as His friend. Not a fair-weather friend. Not a casual acquaintance or professional colleague. He isn't a network connection, occasional companion, or buddy. He is a faithful, forever friend. He sticks closer than a brother. He laid down His life for you.

God stands outside of time and weighs every minute of our life in the scales of eternity. There He pours in His divine love, allowing us to know Him in this friend dimension so He can pull us closer still and there reveal our identity as His beloved daughters and sons.

At last I was ready to experience God not just as Creator or Savior, not only as Master and Friend. I was now ready to shed every remnant of my orphan spirit and get to know God as Father.

ENDNOTES

1. Song of Songs 2:12, TPT.
2. See John 15:15.
3. See 1 John 1:5.
4. See Proverbs 14:1.
5. See Proverbs 14:12.
6. See Psalm 103:12.
7. See James 4:8.
8. Psalm 27:8, 11, 13, 14, NLT.
9. Bill Johnson is the Senior Leader of Bethel Church in Redding, California.
10. Romans 12:1-2, TPT.
11. Jim Rohn is an American entrepreneur, world-renowned author, and motivational speaker.

It was time to for me to experience all that delights God's heart. It was time for a total transformation of how I thought. I was ready to live a beautiful life—satisfying and perfect in His eyes.

Daughter

Chapter Six

DAUGHTER

*Can you not discern this new day of
destiny breaking forth around you?*

*The early signs of purpose and
plans are bursting forth.*

*The budding vines of new life are
now blooming everywhere.*

*The fragrance of their flowers whispers,
"There is change in the air."*

*Arise, my love, my beautiful companion,
and run with me to a higher place.*

*For now is the time to arise
and come away with me.*[1]

THE BRIDEGROOM KING

I grew up hearing statements like "God is a good Father" all the time. In Catholic school, we recited "Our Father" daily, but I never understood the full reality of what that meant to me in tangible terms. Then I read verses like, "See what great love the Father has lavished on us, that we should be called children of God!"[2] and "So you are no longer a [servant], but God's child; and since you are His child, God has made you also an heir."[3]

I continued to grow in my relationship with God. I had transformed my view of a servant as a bad thing—lowly, poor, and without options, and I now viewed serving as a privilege and a joy. Being God's servant gave me access to His family and household! And then, as I went deeper and became more intimate with Him, I ventured into the beautiful reality of friendship with God. This allowed me to experience Him in a whole new dimension. As God's friend, I got to sit with Him at the table, not just prepare it. I got to enter and participate in the conversation, not just be in proximity to overhear it.

Friendship with God was exciting and wonderful, but now I felt Holy Spirit drawing me closer still—no longer just a servant or friend, I was actually God's child. Chosen. Born of the Spirit. An heir. A joint heir with Jesus.

Wow!

Now a [servant] has no permanent place in the family, but a son (daughter) belongs to it forever.[4]

The words penetrated my heart. In India, masters can dismiss their servants at any time for no reason, even if they have served them for decades. Servants can walk away from their masters at any time they want. So being a servant is always tenuous, a temporary, non-binding relationship. Servants are accepted in the family but never really belong to it. Children, however, belong forever. Parents sacrifice for their children. They provide for them. Educate. Clothe. Feed. Nurture. Being a child—even a child who serves their parents—is a very different reality than being a servant. The bond is unbreakable. My spirit reached to grasp the magnitude of what it meant to be a child of the Creator of the universe! It was incomprehensible.

Overwhelming.

In the beginning, where time began, God created male and female *in His image*! He lovingly crafted us as members of His own family, bearing His likeness. God rules and reigns over the entire cosmos. He gave us the authority and responsibility to have dominion over the earth—the fish, fowl, livestock, forests, deserts, plains ... As His children, we reign over His creation![5]

I had been taught the story of creation as a child. I had memorized what was created on each day. I know the factoids like they were answers to trivia questions. As an adult believer, I gave the idea of God as Father some mental assent. I embraced the concept generally—after all, we are all God's children. So, in that sea of humans populating the planet, if we are *all* children of God, then how special could that really be?

Being God's daughter was just information to me. It was something I knew about God. It was not something I had experienced with Him yet. But now that I was beginning to know Him as my friend—funny, involved, conversational, a living and breathing part of my daily life—I could begin to reach for the truth of experiencing Him as my heavenly Father. Not just a distant benevolent being responsible for seven billion people on the planet, but as a loving, invested, caring Father to me.

> **The truth that I was God's child began to shake loose any hold the kingdom of darkness had left in my heart.**

The truth of this began to shake loose any hold the kingdom of darkness had left in my heart.

I was God's child. I was His daughter!

From the time I was a small child, I always worked hard to prove myself. I had to do all the right things not to disgrace the family. To be a daughter, I needed to pull my weight. Do my chores. Get good grades. I needed the approval and recognition of being at the top. I constantly fought to be better than someone else—anyone else, really. I needed to be number one. In my career, I needed to be a top earner. A top producer. Respected. Needed. Valuable because of my skills and performance.

My whole identity was wrapped in achievement. I needed to earn my place, so I was constantly striving, never at rest.

I was exhausted.

I had no idea how tired I really was. A lifetime of proving yourself drains you of vitality.

Then I met Kerry and Chiqui Wood. Together they pastor the Table of Friends Church, disciple leadership couples, and teach at various Christian universties. They introduced me to the concept of an orphan spirit—deeply embedded fears of being rejected, punished, or overlooked by God. An orphan spirit drives you to prove yourself—prove your value and your worth; take care of yourself; look out for yourself; comfort yourself; provide for yourself.

The opposite spirit is sonship. From them, I learned that a son (child) has nothing to fear, nothing to prove, nothing to lose, and nothing to hide.

This concept sounds so simple, but the paradigm of performance was so deeply ingrained in my belief system that it took a miraculous transformation by Holy Spirit to free me from an orphan spirit mentality and embrace the spirit of sonship.

"Lord," I prayed aloud, "please get this orphan spirit out of me!"

"Daddy," I tried it out. It felt awkward and weird. Somehow almost fake to my ears, but I addressed Him again, "Daddy, please take away this orphan spirit and help me understand and embrace the very essence of who I am in You."

From that prayer on, I began to call God "Daddy" whenever and wherever I could. Sometimes it felt forced or contrived. Not natural, and I was tempted to revert to the more formal "Father" or "Father God" title. But when I approached Him with that formality, I noticed that it altered the intimacy of my approach, so I became very intentional in calling Him "Daddy." I had to train my mind to think differently[6] until conversations with Daddy became more natural and easy.

You see, daughters think differently than servants or friends. Daughters have a certain entitlement, not in the negative, spoiled brat way, but in the security, identity, and privilege of belonging to the family and being a member of the household. A servant may access the refrigerator when instructed to do so or as part of fulfilling their duties to the master. A friend may access the refrigerator when invited or by asking, "May I please ...?"

Daughters think differently than servants or friends.

However, a daughter can come into the kitchen, open the refrigerator door, and help herself to what is inside. She doesn't need special permission and will not get in trouble for helping herself to the provisions inside. She has been authorized to eat what she wants from the abundant supply provided by her loving parents.

I realized the orphan spirit mentality had me locked into the servant dynamic. I felt timid and shy to approach God and ask Him for anything as if it was a violation of my station or might cross the line and make Him find me ungrateful or unfaithful. In some ways, I was still approaching God as an outsider because I did not feel I had the freedom to access the bounty of heaven's resources. I still felt like I had to earn them. I could be "paid" in favor and blessings for my "service" (obedience). Even as I grew more comfortable calling God "Daddy," this belief system was still operating at my core.

Holy Spirit gently prodded and provoked me. Whenever I responded as an orphan, He would highlight that I was operating in an orphan spirit and invite me out. There was no condemnation or blame; He simply showed me, "This is where you are, Yvonne, but I will lead you out of this." He spoke truth to my heart, replacing every lie I had believed for a lifetime.

At first, the transformation began slowly, almost incident by incident. But gradually, the lies relinquished their hold on my heart, and as truth grew brighter and clearer, I became a confident child with godly self-esteem and an awareness of the authority I carried. I remember the day when I finally knew, "I can walk around without makeup! I don't need a mask. I don't need to pretend or put on a show. I can be authentically me—I am accepted and adored as I am!" It was very freeing.

"I am your Father—your Daddy," God spoke to my heart.

"You certainly are," I responded, joy overflowing. For the first time, I understood what it meant when Jesus called Him Abba. It was personal. It was intimate and close, not distant, or formal, or far away. Calling God Daddy now came naturally.

I *belonged* on the inside—a permanent residence of abiding. I can serve my Daddy because I love Him so much I long to please Him, and it brings me joy to delight Him. Whatever He asks of me, I will gladly say, "Yes!" I can be friends with my Daddy because we have a special relationship—inside jokes, our own special language, and experiences with each other that are private and meaningful. We share an unbreakable bond. I can tell Him *a-n-y-t-h-i-n-g,* and He will not turn His face from me.

I began to see myself—who I really am—in light of who He is, and that changed everything!

Now, whenever the old nature tries to reassert itself or the orphan spirit rears its ugly head, I get back on course quickly by asking myself these four questions:

Am I trying to hide something?

Am I trying to prove something?

Am I fearful of something?

Am I afraid of losing something?

If the answer to any of these is yes, I know I am not responding as God's daughter. I have slipped back into an orphan mentality. The remedy is to quickly confront whatever I am trying to hide, prove, be afraid of, or fear losing and chat with Daddy about that. He always listens, and He always removes the fear and shame.

Holy Spirit always guides me into all truth.[7]

When I was born, my parents named me Shalini Yvonne D'Souza. That was my official, legal name. However, as in many cultures, children are given nicknames, and I was no exception. When I was little, my older sister Roshni started calling me Bulla, and to this day, my family calls me Bulla. It is a term of endearment to them.

When I went to Catholic school, I used my given name, Shalini. This is how I was known in the community—at church, school, and among our friends.

When we moved to Montreal, I had to attend a French-speaking high school. All my teachers were French, and classes were all taught in French. It seemed no one could pronounce the name Shalini properly, so in an effort to make their lives (and mine) easier, I suggested that they could use my middle name. "Just call me Yvonne," I offered. The name Yvonne is French in origin, so it quickly caught on, and Shalini was soon forgotten.

When I got married, I released my maiden name D'Souza and took on Paul's last name, Allen. My marriage certificate, college degree, passport, driver's license, and all major documents transitioned to Yvonne S. Allen.

"*Bulla*, what would you like to eat when you visit?" my mom asked.

"*Shalini*, when are you coming back to visit Mumbai?" my friends *WhatsApped* from India.

"*Yvonne,* what are you closing in loans this month?" my boss emailed.

"*Mom*, I need to get some new pants for school," my son informed me.

"*Sweetheart*, you look beautiful!" my husband whispered.

So many different names!

All of them are me. All the names fit me in different roles, but I always wondered what my heavenly Father—my Daddy—called me.

I meditated on this scripture:

> And I will give you treasures hidden in the darkness—secret riches. I will do this so you may know that I am the Lord, God of Israel, **the one who calls you by name**.[8]

"Daddy, what do You call me?" I asked. "What is Your favorite name for me? Is it Bulla? Shalini? Yvonne? Something else?"

One night, I came across this passage in Isaiah:

> The nations will see your vindication, and all the kings your glory; **you will be called by a new name that the Lord will bestow**.
>
> You will be a crown of splendor in the Lord's hand, a royal diadem in the hand of your God.
>
> No longer will they call you Deserted, or name your land Desolate.
>
> But you will be called Hephzibah, and your land **Beulah**; for the Lord will take delight in you, and your land will be married.
>
> As a young man marries a maiden, so will your sons marry you; as a bridegroom rejoices over his bride, so will your God rejoice over you.[9]

I was excited for two reasons. The first was because I saw a form of my name, "Beulah," in scripture—pronounced almost the same. The second was because I read that I would be called by a new name that the Lord would bestow.

"So, what do You call me, Daddy?" I asked again, this time expecting an answer!

One Friday in June, we visited friends to celebrate Shabbat with them. After dinner, we prayed together, and Ana said, "I don't know why, but I keep hearing the word 'Hephzibah.' The Father calls you 'Hephzibah,' and He gives you this new name which means, 'My delight is in you!'"

My spirit leaped for joy! I recalled the Isaiah passage, "But you will be called **Hephzibah**, and your land Beulah; for **the Lord will take delight in you!**"

I had told no one of my desire to know what name Daddy God had given me. I had not even told Paul about finding a form of my name in scripture and claiming the promise that the Lord would give me a new name. I had only asked Daddy about this.

Tears streamed down my face as my friends and Paul looked on. "He calls me *Hephzibah*!" I exclaimed, "My name is *Hephzibah*!"

Together, we looked up the Isaiah passage and read it aloud. There was the promise that the Lord would give me a new name. There was my nickname (Beulah), and there was the promised new name, Hephzibah—the Lord takes delight in me!

Unspeakable joy flooded my soul as God's love overwhelmed me.

Unspeakable joy flooded my soul as God's love overwhelmed me. It consumed me.

A few weeks later, a friend messaged me and said, "While I was praying for you, Daddy told me that your middle name is 'Father's Joy.'"

Once again, I was taken aback. My cup overflowed. I had asked for a name, and He gave me two!

"Daddy, I cannot contain all the love You are pouring into me!" Then I thought, "If You have a first name for me and a middle name for me, You must have a last name for me, too!"

I was not in a hurry about it. I was not demanding or impatient. I just knew that God had a complete name for me. I was blissfully wrapped in Daddy's arms. I snuggled into His *kolpos*—the bosom of His garment, close to His heart. There was nothing anyone could say to me; there was no circumstance that could occur that could snatch me from His arms. I was safe. Secure. Full of love, joy, and peace.

About six months later, I attended the First Conference at our church. A random stranger sat next to me, and out of nowhere, with no introduction or preface, he said, "The Lord sees you as 'Committed.' It's like your last name is 'Committed.'"

I'm sure I stared at him, mouth open, eyes wide. I was in complete awe. The very *last* thing I saw myself as was *committed*! I tried so hard to be disciplined and committed, but I felt as if I always fell short of the standard. But here was this stranger providing the answer to my private prayer for God to share how He saw me and what last name He gave me. "Committed," I pondered, "my last name is Committed."

"That's *really* how You see me?" I asked.

"It sure is," He answered.

Finally, the pieces of the puzzle began to connect in my heart. Daddy had given me this name:

- **Hephzibah** (My delight is in you!)
- **Father's Joy** (You delight Me, too!)
- **Committed** (You are wholeheartedly dedicated and loyal to Me, as I am to you!)

I tried the name on.

It fit me to a tee!

"You're never gonna let, never gonna let me do-own," we repeated the song lyrics again and again during worship. Long after worship ended and the sermon was going on, the lyrics stayed with me. The same belief system and thought patterns that once bound me to approach God as an orphan had one last thread still clinging to my soul.

I had made a point of measuring my expectations with people so that I wouldn't be disappointed. If I didn't expect anything from them (or not much from them), then they wouldn't let me down. During this morning's worship service, it dawned on me that I had the same "measured expectations" with God. It wasn't that I had no expectations of Him, but I didn't want any expectation that was too high, so I wouldn't have an opportunity to become disappointed with Him.

I didn't verbalize these thoughts; after all, Pastor Robert was still preaching. But Holy Spirit interrupted them just the same. Lovingly but with strength, He said, "You can have high expectations of Me. I am the Creator of the universe! So yes, Hephzibah, you can certainly have high expectations of Me."

Boldness welled up inside my spirit. My confidence grew. Yes, God is my Father—my Daddy, and He is a good, good Father. Nothing is impossible for Him. How dare I limit my expectations of His ability or power or intention toward me!

This experience taught me to pray and keep on praying no matter what the circumstance looked like, no matter what the outcome. I must trust Daddy completely. If my expectations were too low, then my faith could not be activated. Did I believe His Word? Did I trust Him?

He reminded me:

> So shall My word be that goes forth from My mouth. It shall not return to Me void, but it shall accomplish what I please, and it shall prosper in the thing for which I sent it.[10]

Little by little. Line upon line. Precept upon precept, my mind was being renewed, and my heart was being transformed.

Not long after, God gave me the opportunity to test out my newly minted high expectations of Him. At about 4:00 in the afternoon, a severe thunderstorm began to build. Now, thunderstorms in Texas are a magnificent thing to behold. They roll in across the prairie without the hindrance of mountains or hills to slow them down. The lightning is fierce, the thunder intense. Rain can fall as if someone opened a swimming pool over your head, and balls of hail can pile up like snow in a matter of minutes.

Paul was flying home from Boston, and a storm caused his flight to be rerouted to Oklahoma for safety. But our daughter, Rebekah, and I were already sitting at the Dallas/Fort Worth airport, awaiting his arrival. As we sat in the baggage claim at about 4:30 pm, we got a notice that his flight was no longer landing at DFW. So, we went back to the car and started heading home.

At 5:27 pm, Holy Spirit prompted me that I could declare and decree a thing[11] and take authority over the situation. He invited me to speak out the outcome I desired.

So, with Rebekah sitting in the passenger seat beside me, I mustered up all the authority I could manage and boldly declared, "Paul's flight *will* take off from Oklahoma City and land at DFW before 7:00 pm *today*!"

We are pretty experienced travelers, so I know that a weather system creates havoc for travelers. Many, many planes must be rerouted and refueled. Stranded passengers scramble to fly on standby to resolve canceled and delayed flights. The last time something like this happened, Paul was rerouted to Oklahoma City; he didn't arrive in DFW until 3:00 am the next morning. But I put all that aside, made my bold declaration, and dared to raise my expectations. Rebekah agreed with my prayer, and together we shouted, *"Amen!"*

I kept driving, and Rebekah opened the Flight Tracker app on her phone. This app allows you to follow a specific flight and track the plane in progress to a given destination.

"Mom!" Rebekah exclaimed, "Look! There it is!"

A massive miracle was taking place right in front of our eyes. It showed that Paul's plane was being refueled. A few minutes later, at 6:00, his flight left OKC and headed for DFW!

Paul landed at exactly 6:52 pm. Eight minutes earlier than I had boldly declared.

I smiled big, showing all my teeth. "You exceeded my expectations, Daddy—and they were pretty high!"

I no longer acquiesce to circumstances that seem immovable. I no longer just *go with the flow*. Daddy taught me that I can *establish the flow* as Holy Spirit leads me. When I partner with what He is saying, it will manifest. It is as simple as that.

As my fortieth birthday approached, I didn't want a party or a special vacation; I wanted to go on a mission trip—by myself, without Paul or the kids. I let Daddy know about my desire.

I received an email from Dr. Chiqui Wood inviting friends to partner with her on a mission trip to Egypt sponsored by Gateway Women.

"Paul," I called out, "Paul, Chiqui is going on a mission trip to Egypt. Would you mind if I went along?"

"Ask the Lord," he replied. (Typical Paul!)

The next morning at my favorite Central Market corner table, I sat down with Daddy and asked, "Should I go to Cairo with Gateway Women in November?"

No answer. I heard nothing.

I went to the office and began checking my email. There were so many that needed to be answered! Among them was our internal office email, sent out at 9:51 that morning—the weekly devotional. I confess I don't always read these emails, but the subject line caught my eye. It said, "You asked for a sign." So, I clicked open the email and thought, *Okay, if Egypt is mentioned in this email, then that is a sign I should go to Cairo on this mission trip.*

I skimmed through the email, honestly not really paying attention to the encouraging lesson; I was on a word hunt for "Egypt." It was there—not once, but two times it appeared. It was not a term normally found in our inter-office communications, so this was no mere coincidence. I had asked Daddy for a sign, and He gave me one.

I answered Chiqui:

9:59 am—Me: Saw your email regarding the mission trip to Egypt. Any chance I could join you?

11:55 am—Chiqui: It would be awesome! I think the trip is full, but let me check.

12:20 pm—Me: I was asking God this morning for a confirmation if I should go to Egypt, and He said, "Yes." Will share it with you soon.

I waited for her reply, but it wasn't instant. I kept checking the Gateway Missions website, as I had done since I first got confirmation from the Lord, but it said the trip was full. The application process was closed. An hour went by, and I still had no word from her.

I checked the website again, and it said, "Apply Now," so I did! *If Daddy said yes, then no one else can say no,* I thought.

1:39 pm—Chiqui: Well, I just heard that someone dropped out this morning, and there is a spot. I am sending you a link right now for you to apply ASAP. Check your email.

1:40 pm—Me: I just went online and completed an application a few minutes ago.

1:42 pm—Chiqui: Yay! They just opened it up for you—literally. The trip was closed, and they opened it because I asked about you going. How cool is that?

1:43 pm—Me: God is good. What a miracle!

Beyond a shadow of a doubt, I know God orchestrated this, but a bigger miracle was yet to come. He wanted me to stretch my expectations of Him further. You see, I could afford to pay for the trip outright. It was not a hardship. In fact, I would happily have contributed to others going. But Daddy instructed me that He would provide the money for this trip outside my control. It was not something I was to do because I had earned it. He had another way.

On top of that, He instructed me that I was not to ask for financial support. I needed to trust Him that He would take care of it. Orphans make their own way—daughters receive gifts.

A month later, a couple heard from God that they were to sow $1,000 toward my trip. They obeyed and brought me cash.

"Okay, Daddy. Thank You! I was really starting to wonder if You had forgotten Your promise to me, but here is $1,000 that I did not ask for." Still, I struggled. I had moments of extreme faith followed by moments of questioning. I was tempted just to write a check and pay for the trip and then allow God to "pay me back" whenever He was ready.

I had moments of extreme faith followed by moments of questioning.

But that was not what He said. He told me to wait. He told me not to lift a finger but to trust Him to provide.

A few more weeks passed. Then it was a month. I grew anxious and called the trip coordinator to confirm that I had not missed the deadline to pay for the trip. I wanted to remind Daddy that the clock was ticking!

A few more weeks passed, and the deadline to pay in full expired. Now I felt embarrassed—I always paid my bills on time. Not just on time, but early. I paid whatever I owed—always. I felt like my reputation was on the line here, and I grew agitated.

I journaled about it, acknowledging the deadline—the *missed* deadline—and then thanked Daddy for providing the whole amount as He promised He would.

Nothing happened.

A few days later, I asked Him, "Is it okay if I just pay the balance? Or can I at least post about it on Facebook or something and ask for support?"

"No," He answered, "I haven't changed My mind. You must trust Me."

That afternoon, a friend from Boston texted me to ask when I was leaving for Egypt. "I was hoping I hadn't missed it," she said, "for a few weeks, I have felt like the Lord wanted me to give toward the trip, but I am just now getting around to it. I want to send you some money."

"Wonderful—thank you!" I exclaimed and gratefully received the provision.

But a balance remained.

A few more weeks passed, and I was growing concerned that they might not allow me to go since I had not yet paid for my trip. I went to speak with Dr. Kerry Wood, a spiritual dad to me.

"Kerry," I began, "Daddy said He would provide the funds for this trip. He clearly instructed me that I should not raise funds or pay for it myself. But the deadline has come and gone, and I have only a little over a third of the money required to go."

"Yvonne, I want to say two things," he replied, "First, you need to rest. His yoke is easy, and His burden is light. Second, has anyone from the mission trip committee asked you for funds?"

"No," I answered. Honestly, that felt a little strange to me.

"Well," Kerry said, "then why are you concerned? It has already been established that this is not your bill—it's His. I'm pretty sure He is aware of the deadlines. He will come through."

I took Kerry at his word and decided to rest and release it. It was true, no one had asked me for funds, and it was not my bill to pay.

So, I thanked Daddy for His gift and went on about my business. I found that sweet place of rest and peace, and now instead of being anxious about it, I began to anticipate how He was going to pull it off. I wondered how He would provide.

My birthday approached, and Paul planned a surprise party for me. It was wonderful—friends gathered to celebrate, they prayed over me, and spoke prophetic words and blessings over me. I was so overwhelmed. I received another $1,000 for the trip through gifts and gratefully thanked God for the supply. But there was still a $900 shortfall.

Once again, I asked the Lord if He wanted me to ask for support or if I could just write myself a check to cover the balance. Once again, He said nothing.

So, I did nothing. Nothing but wait.

I got a text while I was out of town. My friend, Mary Grace, told me she received a card in the mail addressed to me. I told her I would meet her for coffee sometime when I returned. Then I forgot about it.

We were now just two weeks out from departure to Egypt, and Mary Grace sent me an email reminding me she still had a card meant for me, so we got together the next day. We sat down at Starbucks, and she handed me the envelope as we sat and talked. I began to feel excited. I felt strongly that the rest of the funds for my trip were in that card!

I tried to keep myself focused on my friend, but finally, I could take the anticipation no longer, and I tried to (as nonchalantly as possible) open the card. There was another miracle right in front of my eyes! A check for $5,000 was in that envelope, and when I saw it, I began to cry. Mary Grace asked, "Is everything okay?"

"Okay?" I stammered, "everything is *more* than *okay*! My God is a God of more than enough!" I filled her in on the details of letting

Daddy pay for the trip—and how this check went above and beyond the need. Daddy had sent me way more than I needed!

It was perfect timing for her, as she needed to be reminded that God would supply her needs and that God is extravagant and generous. He honors stewardship. He honors faith. He has compassion for our needs. When Jesus fed the multitudes, everyone ate their fill, and there was no lack. Daddy had come through for me once again.

I tend to be very generous—like my Daddy, but I am still learning when to give and when to do nothing. I am often moved by compassion at the mention of a need, and sometimes I want to act so quickly that it doesn't allow someone else the opportunity to obey. And sometimes, the need is there as a means for God's kindness to lead someone to repentance. If I step in and make them comfortable, they might not turn to Him as He desires. My generosity could actually delay their destiny. So, it is important that I listen and move *only* when He tells me to.

One Sunday, Pastor Robert Morris used an illustration about giving his daughter his credit card while she was away attending college. She used the card for necessities as authorized, but as he examined the statement, he saw that she was using it to treat her friends at restaurants and buy them gifts, so he had to address the issue with her. "Sweetie, just because I gave you my card doesn't mean you can use it whenever and wherever for whatever you like."

His words landed. I heard God say, "Just because You have My credit card, Yvonne, doesn't mean you can use it any time you like. You need to use it in partnership with My desires. You must be led by Holy Spirit."

Yes, God owns the cattle on a thousand hills. Everything belongs to Him. Yes, I am His daughter, and I am a beneficiary of His goodness—a signer on His accounts. He has unlimited resources, and through this sermon illustration, it sunk in that God had given me His credit card. I had access to those unlimited resources—and He wanted me to be trustworthy with them, to operate as a faithful and wise steward, and use them according to His desires.

I am His daughter, His beneficiary, a signer on His accounts ...

I was overwhelmed by the generosity this represented and the responsibility required to steward His resources. Being His daughter began to take on a new dimension.

When I encounter people we are discipling or mentoring, and I am made aware they are burdened by debt, I still think, "I can just pay this off for them and take care of it right now." But I have learned to sit on that for a day or two and ask Holy Spirit what His desire is. My funds are His. I will release them to whomever He tells me to give them to. Sometimes He says, "Give," and I get the joy of participating in their miracle.

Sometimes, He says, "Walk beside them," and we come alongside them as they work, save up, pay off their debt, become generous, and grow in wisdom and strength. It might sound odd to say that sometimes compassion is the thought I must take captive, but it's true. Compassion can move me to step outside the will of the Father and do a good thing that turns out to be the wrong thing.

When Daddy DOES let me use His credit card to bless someone, it is always such fun! For example, a friend from Brazil had a pie-making business in Boston. She was just starting out—a single mom with three sons, working hard to make ends meet and stepping into the entrepreneurial arena with a dream, a plan, and a solid work ethic.

My friend asked me for nothing, but Holy Spirit told me to send her a check for $5,000. I have a play account where I save money so I can give when God prompts me to, and I always use Paul as my sounding board when I feel the urge. I asked Paul how he felt about it, and He was neutral. Generally, when I feel prompted to give a large sum, I sleep on it to see if the desire lingers for a few days. If I forget about it and it doesn't come up in my spirit again, then I release it. But this desire grew, so I mailed her a check.

It came at just the right time! She needed to purchase some equipment to scale the business, and now her products are in grocery stores! God supplied her need and allowed me the privilege to be His hands and feet to get the provision to her.

In business, people always have a title on their business cards—Chief Financial Officer, Account Executive, Manager, etc. It is the same thing in ministry—Pastor, Associate Pastor, Bishop, Evangelist, etc. "Daddy," I said one day, "I need a title. What's my title?"

I was preparing to go to Armenia on a mission trip, and the pastors from several large churches where I would minister kept asking for my title so they could print flyers for the meetings. I asked again, "Daddy, what's my title?"

He answered, "You are My daughter, and you are My witness."

This was confirmed one weekend while walking a trail where He spoke clearly, "You shall preach to the nations; I have called you to be my daughter and a witness."

The next time I was asked what my title was, I proudly answered, "The Father says I'm His daughter and His witness." I am completely secure in this reality. I need nothing more.

I have a relationship with my Daddy, unlike the one I have with my earthly father. No topic is off-limits. I know who I am and can come to Him boldly, without timidity. I don't have to be guarded or pretend I am together when I am not. Being God's daughter means I never have to fear being dismissed, let go, or cast out.

- As an **insider**, I timidly hung in the outer court, just grateful to be allowed inside.

- As a **servant**, I grew comfortable in the surroundings. I learned the ways of my Master, I picked up on His language and customs, His likes and dislikes, and I enjoyed the access and took pleasure in obeying Him. I liked bringing Him joy.

- As His **friend**, I relished sitting with Him at the table. I learned to fellowship with Him and get to know His personality. I experienced His sense of humor and playfulness. I grew more confident in sharing my secrets with Him. I talked to Him less formally and felt acceptance I had never before experienced.

- As I entered the blessings of sonship, I began to experience God as my Father, as my Daddy, and the kingdom of heaven began to open up before me. There were vast rooms to explore, and as His **daughter**, I was allowed to go into every single one! I now have a deep level of trust and wave upon wave of love. I marvel at His goodness, His extravagance, and His great grace and mercy. I learned I was not an orphan, but a beloved child—His favorite!

Little did I know that another dimension was waiting for me to explore. My journey from outsider to insider to servant to friend to daughter still had something more for me to experience. It was time for me to enter a season of preparation where I would become His bride.

ENDNOTES

1. Song of Songs 2:13, TPT.
2. 1 John 3:1, NIV.
3. Galatians 4:7, NIV. [Servant] used instead of slave.
4. John 8:35, NIV. [Servant] used instead of slave, parenthesis added.
5. See Genesis 1:26-31.
6. See Romans 12:2, 2 Corinthians 10:5.
7. See John 16:13.
8. Isaiah 45:3, NLT, emphasis added.
9. Isaiah 62:2-4, NIV, emphasis added.
10. Isaiah 55:11, NKJV.
11. See Job 22:28.

Bride

Chapter Seven

BRIDE

*For you are my dove, hidden
in the split-open rock.
It was I who took you and hid you up
high in the secret stairway of the sky.
Let me see your radiant face
and hear your sweet voice.
How beautiful your eyes of worship
and lovely your voice in prayer.*[1]

THE BRIDEGROOM KING

There she stands, clothed in pure white. She has prepared herself with great care. The day she has dreamt about since she was a small girl has finally arrived. Her bridegroom waits for her, and when her father has walked her down the aisle and delivered her to him, they proceed with a covenant ceremony. Every word has layers rich in purpose and deep with meaning. The veil. The vows. The rings. Each minute draws them closer and closer to the moment when they seal the covenant with a kiss, and they become joined.

There is a great wedding feast and celebration. Everyone they know has gathered to witness, clothed in their very best to mark the occasion. The tables are laden with food. The setting is extravagant and opulent; no expense has been spared. There is careful thought in the placement of every plate, napkin, utensil, and goblet. From the beautiful floral arrangements to the lighting to the music, every part of this atmosphere has been crafted with love and intention.

Let us rejoice and be glad and give Him glory!

For the wedding of the Lamb has come, and His bride has made herself ready.

Fine linen, bright and clean, was given her to wear ...

Blessed are those who are invited to the wedding supper of the Lamb![2]

Then, as the guests finish the final course of their gourmet banquet, the bridesmaids enter and begin to dance. The bride joins them. There is joy and laughter, and each is beautiful and comely, but the groom has eyes only for her. His gaze is locked on his beloved, and he sees no one else in the room. She dances for him and him alone. Her beauty is more radiant because he basks in its glow. His pledge to honor, protect, provide for, and defend is written on his face. His heart trusts in her, and her heart is wholly his—undivided.

Later they will steal away, and the two will become one. Flesh of flesh. Bone of bone. They will be fruitful and multiply.

Throughout the Bible, the bride of Christ is a metaphor used to describe the Church and its relationship with Jesus. As metaphors go, it is imperfect, but it does help convey the invitation to intimacy with Christ we so often miss when we give our heart to Him.

I opened this chapter with a picture of a wedding I attended in Armenia. I was overcome by the celebration, and the bridesmaids and bride danced just as I described. As they danced, there was smoke and fireworks and bubbles, and it was the most jubilant celebration I could imagine. As I watched, Holy Spirit said, "Look at the bride! Look at the groom! Watch how they look at each other!"

It took my breath away. With all the joy and merriment surrounding them, they were oblivious to everything except each other. His eyes were only on her. Her eyes were only on him. Their desire to slip away and be enraptured in each other's arms was unmistakable. "For your Maker is your Husband, the Lord of hosts is His name,"[3] suddenly came alive in my spirit! As the bride of Christ, we must fix our eyes upon Jesus because He has never taken His eyes off us.

He is not returning for a servant, a friend, or a child. Jesus is coming back for His bride—a mature Church who has prepared herself for Him. She is ready to present herself without spot or blemish or wrinkle, but holy and blameless in all her glory saved for Him alone.

Jesus is not returning for a servant, friend, or child—He is coming back for His bride!

Consider this: friends of a bridegroom may attend the wedding. They may attend to the groom, standing with him. Servants aid in the preparation of the feast. Both may come and go from the groom's home, but they do not own the house. The groom may leave a portion of an inheritance to His servants, friends, and sons—but his bride has it all. Her name is on every deed. She is a signer on every account. What is his is also hers.

We are the bride of Christ. What is His is also ours.

Shortly after our move to Dallas, Paul and I began a covenant friendship with a woman named Cynthia Peaslee. We were just beginning to get to know one another when God had her send me— very much still a daughter in my relationship with God—a message. This is what it said:

> *Paul, I don't have your wife's phone number, but boy, God has been putting her on my heart today. Please share this with her. My heart is pounding with joy from this message. I feel the love of her beloved Jesus! He is the lover of her soul. He says to her:*
>
> *"I am in love with you. You are beautiful to Me.*
>
> *I look at your beauty and am in awe. Yes, I am in awe.*
>
> *I am enamored by your grace.*
>
> *All those around you see your beauty because I am greater in you than you are in yourself.*
>
> *I call you favored, oh Beloved!*
>
> *I gaze at you with great delight. I am pleased with you. I see you. I cannot keep My eyes off you.*
>
> *I see you. I see you.*

Your children call you blessed.

You are the epitome of beauty in every way.

For your heart is pure and undefiled with thanksgiving, and I see your generosity.

You love others as I love them; You see them as I see them.

I am in love with you, oh Beloved; you are Mine and I am surely pleased with you."

Her text continued:

Yes, Them. I felt all were looking at you! (Father, Jesus, and Holy Spirit) One last thing I am supposed to tell you (you may already know). Chains are broken. All things are being made new again. Generational strongholds and curses are demolished.

I felt as if I had been passed an intimate love note in class. The message was so much to take in—I didn't know where to start! Before that, I did not realize how Father, Son, and Holy Spirit perceived me. As I read this message over and over again, my perception began to shift. My attitude changed. My mind was renewed, and my heart was transformed as it began to beat in sync with His. Slowly, just as I had passed from servant to daughter, I began to pass from daughter to fiancé. I was like a giddy schoolgirl—in the beginning stages of wonder and curiosity as infatuation yields to love. I was in love with Jesus.

The Creator of the universe took the time to pass me a love note. I listen for and hear His voice. We often have conversations together, but I also love getting prophetic words—confirmation and affirmation through another. So in His kindness, He sent His message to me through a friend. His words were like cold, clear, spring water on a hot Texas day. They quenched my thirst and satisfied my soul. What joy it was to be pursued and courted. How affirming that He delighted in me and desired that I should delight in Him!

I responded to His invitation quickly, just as Abigail responded to David's call:

> *Then David sent messengers to Abigail to ask her to become his wife. When the messengers arrived at Carmel, they told Abigail, "David has sent us to take you back to marry him."*
>
> *She bowed low to the ground and responded, "I, your servant, would be happy to marry David. I would even be willing to become a slave, washing the feet of his servants!"*
>
> *Quickly getting ready, she took along five of her servant girls as attendants, mounted her donkey, and went with David's messengers. And so, she became his wife.*[4]

So, I said yes to Him, but "the heart cannot love what the mind does not know."[5] I could regard Him. I could be devoted to Him and adore Him, but I could not truly love Him until I took the time to get to know Him. I longed to know what He loved. What does He hate? What breaks His heart? What causes Him to rejoice? What pleases Him? What makes Him laugh?

When Paul courted me, my curiosity about his character and personality was insatiable. I wanted to know everything about him. I wanted to know what his favorite food was, and if he preferred coffee or tea. I wanted to know his favorite color—and why it was his favorite. Finding out was half the fun. Each time we were together was a joyful encounter of discovery.

Until that point in my relationship with God, I had encountered Him more through the experience of others than by experiencing Him for myself. I had been content to live on milk—nutrition that had broken down and provided for me by the digestion of another. Now it was time for me to mature and begin to eat the meat of His Word. It was time for me to learn how to hear His voice with my ears and to discern His heart with my spirit. To commune with Him directly and not only in the company of others.

> **It was time for me to mature, to learn how to hear His voice with my ears and discern His heart with my spirit.**

Jesus was courting me (just as Paul had done) by inviting me to dine, by bringing me flowers, and by telling me things I had never before heard. He had numbered the hairs on my head, and my worth to Him was beyond compare.[6] I was fearfully and wonderfully made.[7] I was His poem.[8] I was chosen—royal.[9] Anointed.[10] Christ invited me to be His bride, and I said yes. Now it was time for me to prepare to step into that role.

Dating may provide a shallow level of intimacy—more of a familiarity—but courtship is slow and unhurried. Courtship is pursuit with purpose. Jesus already knew me inside and out. I needed to know Him in ways I had not yet even known to explore.

When Esther prepared to meet the king, she spent six months bathing in the oil of myrrh. Esther lived in a hot, dry desert climate. I imagine her skin showed the effects—cracked and dry. Oil was used for cleansing, purification, and healing. Esther bathed in the oil of myrrh—I bathed in the oil of the Holy Spirit. After Esther was restored and made whole, she spent six more months with perfumes and beautifying herself. This not only provided a pleasing aroma for her king, but it also altered her palette. It trained her senses and elevated them above the common smells of sweat, cooking, and waste in the streets. The process of her preparation brought about a transformation of her identity. She was no longer common. She was fit for a royal household. Like the delicately perfumed Esther, I wanted my life to be a fragrance—to be in the world but not of it. I wanted to be set apart—my identity transformed from common to royal as well.

Even perfume requires preparation. It is made by crushing something. Whether petals or leaves or pods, perfume is extracted only after something has been crushed. The crushing makes it more valuable. In the same way, I came to understand that everything I had endured now had a redemptive purpose. The crushing of my life created the fragrance I bathed myself in to prepare my heart to receive my King.

I began to transition from being a daughter to knowing who I was as His bride. I had to completely change my mindset from that of responding to Him as a child so I could embrace the authority and intimacy of being a wife. I had to put away childish things. I had to mature so I was equipped and ready to administrate the estate of God.

When Esther prepared, she submitted herself to Mordecai and the eunuchs who taught her everything she needed to know to operate in court etiquette—how to speak, how to dress, how to conduct herself—as well as what she would need to please the king in his chamber and find favor in his sight. Esther had to let go of all her previous knowledge and learn the ways of the kingdom for which she had been set apart. Her identity underwent an upgrade.

I went to Proverbs 31. This is the description of a virtuous woman, and there are more teachings about this passage than I can count. But I felt Holy Spirit tell me this was also the description of the bride of Christ. The woman in Proverbs 31 is how Jesus expects His bride to be. He lists many things about her that I began to embrace about myself.

1. **I am more precious than jewels**—valuable and rare.

2. **My Husband trusts me**—I do him good and not evil.

3. **I am industrious**—willing to serve.

4. **I take care of His estate**—procure what is needed, and manage His household.

5. **I am prosperous**—I buy and sell for a profit.

6. **I am strong**—there is nothing feeble about me.

7. **I am generous**—I notice and give to the poor.

8. **I rejoice**—I am clothed in strength and honor.

9. **I am wise**—I give sound counsel, and I am kind.

10. **I am watchful**—aware of myself and those in my charge.

11. **I am worthy of praise**—my children and my Husband bless me; my works bear witness.

12. **I fear the Lord**—I approach Him with holy reverence, and I am in awe of His power, majesty, goodness, grace, mercy, and love.

A passage from Ezekiel spoke to me. In it, God spoke to His covenant people about their condition when He found them and called them to become His bride. I saw myself as I read these words:

On the day you were born, no one cared about you. Your umbilical cord was not cut, and you were never washed, rubbed with salt, and wrapped in cloth. No one had the slightest interest in you; no one pitied you or cared for you. On the day you were born, you were unwanted, dumped in a field, and left to die. But I came by and saw you there, helplessly kicking about in your own blood. As you lay there, I said, 'Live!' And I helped you to thrive like a plant in the field. You grew up and became a beautiful jewel. Your breasts became full, and your body hair grew, but you were still naked. And when I passed by again, I saw that you were old enough for love. So I wrapped my cloak around you to cover your nakedness and declared my marriage vows. I made a covenant with you, says the Sovereign Lord, and you became mine.

Then I bathed you and washed off your blood, and I rubbed fragrant oils into your skin. I gave you expensive clothing of fine linen and silk, beautifully embroidered, and sandals made of fine goatskin leather. I gave you lovely jewelry, bracelets, beautiful necklaces, a ring for your nose, earrings for your ears, and a lovely crown for your head. And so you were adorned with gold and silver. Your clothes were made of fine linen and costly fabric and were beautifully embroidered. You ate the finest foods—choice flour, honey, and olive oil—and became more beautiful than ever. You looked like a queen, and so you were! Your fame soon spread throughout the world because of your beauty. I dressed you in my splendor and perfected your beauty, says the Sovereign Lord.[11]

Can you see how Jesus lovingly prepares us to be His bride? Our part is to cooperate with the process. It is He who makes us without spots or wrinkles or any other blemish. We could never do this on our own, no matter how hard we might try. It is Christ at work within us that allows us to be presented to Him as holy and without fault.[12]

I came to realize that no one was more vested in my preparation as the bride of Christ than Christ Himself. So, I began to make myself available to Him fully, holding nothing back and yielding to His preparation. I surrendered myself—spirit, soul, and body—to His will and His ways in my life. He showed me what I needed to bring with me to His house, and what I needed to leave behind forever.

When a bride's preparations have come to an end, and she is ready to meet her bridegroom, she walks down the aisle to stand with him. Have you ever watched a bride's face as she walks? Even when she wears a veil, you can see her anticipation in every step. Something changes in her as she gets closer and closer to the one she will be joined to. She walks toward him as he stands and waits for her.

In the same way, we must walk toward Jesus. Every step we take is a step of immediate obedience to His Word in our life as it plays out in our daily decisions. And just as a bride does not walk alone, she is escorted by her father for guidance and support; we do not walk alone as we journey to become His bride. He walks beside us—our divine helper, Holy Spirit—with us every step of the way. We walk by faith, not by sight.[13] When we walk by the Spirit, we do not gratify the desires of our flesh.[14] We walk humbly, doing justice and loving mercy.[15] We walk in the way He has commanded us, and when we do, it goes well with us.[16]

But the verse I found myself most excited about came from Zechariah's vision when he saw Joshua, the high priest, standing before the Lord as Satan accused him. Joshua's filthy garments were exchanged for pristine ones as the Lord of hosts told him: "If you will walk in my ways and keep my charge, then you shall rule my house and have charge of my courts, and I will give you the right of access among those who are standing here."[17]

When we spend enough time with Him, He prompts us and lets us know which way and how to walk. For many years, I have prioritized my daily appointment with Holy Spirit. It is often the first appointment of the day when I meet Him at our special booth at Central Market Café. Your special place does not have to look like mine, but if you commit to a place of consistent meeting with Him, He will speak to you and teach you about Himself.

He will call you to walk by the Spirit and learn to walk in His ways. He will guide you to walk humbly, in His light, by faith. Taking these steps is possible only by regular, intimate communion with the Trinity. You must meet with God the Father, Jesus the Son, and Holy Spirit daily. As you spend time in Their presence and begin to carry Their fragrance into "your everyday, ordinary life—your sleeping, eating, going-to-work, and walking-around life,"[18] everything you do becomes a walk down the aisle. You begin to walk toward Jesus with Holy Spirit by your side. Let your anticipation for Him grow. Be intoxicated by His love. Think of Him. Dream of Him. Speak of Him and let His thoughts of you kindle your affection and keep your heart true.

> **As His bride, you walk toward Jesus every day with Holy Spirit by your side.**

I always cry at weddings. I can't help it. The beautiful picture of two people entering into a covenant relationship with each other overwhelms my heart with joy. I'm not the only one. Those who know the couple well can't help but get teary-eyed as the couple repeats their vows, and we celebrate and clap when the officiant declares, "You may now kiss the bride!"

Those moments are precious, indeed! But they would mean nothing and carry no legal weight without the part of the ceremony known as the *Declaration of Intent*. This is when the couple faces each other as the officiant says, "Do you,_____, take _____ to be your lawfully wedded husband/wife?" and they answer, "I do!"

Even if you have a marriage license, have booked a venue, and planned a party, unless you make this specific declaration, the marriage is neither legal nor binding. Isn't that crazy?

It does not matter how beautiful the bride is, how eloquent the vows are, how fancy the flowers are, or how delicious the food is. These things are inconsequential to the ultimate covenant of marriage unless there is a simple, clear, public declaration of intent. It takes mere seconds to say, even though it may take a long, long time to make the decision to say it. Long before the couple makes their public profession, a process began that led their hearts and minds to this place.

You may be familiar with the Scripture, "Thou shalt also decree a thing, and it shall be established unto thee; and the light shall shine upon thy ways."[19] Christians often use this verse as justification to "declare and decree," forgetting that before the words are spoken out loud and established on the outside, they must first be decided and established on the inside.

This is why Paul instructs us to destroy strongholds and arguments that set themselves up against the knowledge of God in our hearts and minds. This is the reason why we must be so diligent to take every thought captive and make it obedient to Christ. Our thoughts become our words. Our words are the decrees we release into the atmosphere, and they have great power. Whether our confession is life or death, health or sickness, unity or discord—it begins in our minds long before we speak the words that become our reality.

Only when you yield your soul and spirit to Holy Spirit do you become aware when your thought patterns do not align with God's Word over you. Strongholds are born in the mind and erected with the mouth. Elisabeth Elliot says this:

Spiritual strongholds begin with a thought. One thought becomes a consideration. A consideration develops into an attitude, which leads then to action. Action repeated becomes a habit, a habit establishes a 'power base for the enemy'—that is a stronghold.

What have you said "I do" to?

What thoughts do you allow free reign inside your soul? What words have become common utterances from your lips? Do they exalt Christ? Do they agree with His mind toward you? Are they pure and lovely and of good report?

Without intentional submission—an active taking of our thoughts captive—we all find ourselves yielding to limiting or harmful ideas and careless or restrictive speech. Learning how to speak His Word over our lives is much more difficult than it sounds. Our thoughts are bombarded daily with complaints, negativity, limitations, entertainment, gossip, bad theology ... and the list goes on. The only way to combat this is to meditate on God's Word, to converse and commune with the Trinity, and to establish our thoughts in what aligns with Him. "So may the words of my mouth, my meditation thoughts, and every movement of my heart be always pure and pleasing, acceptable before your eyes, Yahweh, my only Redeemer, my Protector."[20]

When a bride and groom are physically intimate, they surrender themselves completely to one another. There is nothing held back, no barriers, no masks, no secrets. In the same way, we must learn to surrender all aspects of ourselves to Him—right down to our innermost thoughts. He is safe. We are safe in Him.

Can you pretend?

Yes.

Just as a man and woman can go through all the motions of sexual intercourse without any genuine intimacy—perform the act without connection or union, so can we go through all the motions of Christianity without ever becoming His bride.

I can pick a man at random and Google him. I can learn everything there is to know about him—where he lives and works, his credit score, the deeds to his properties, his tax returns, where he has traveled, whom he is related to, and anything else I care to spend time learning. But that will not make me his wife. Knowing *about* him will give me no authority or access to who he is or what he owns. If I tried to approach him and lay claim to his provision or protection, he would cast me out—"I don't know you. Get away from me!"

Embracing religion without investing in a relationship is nothing more than foolish idolatry.

Embracing religion without investing in a relationship is nothing more than foolish idolatry. It is an exaltation of our will, not a response to the invitation to walk with Him in His will.

We can study the Bible diligently and daily. We can learn all the Bible stories and tenants of the faith, be able to recite doctrine, and have all the impressive religious knowledge. We can quote Scripture in perfect historical and linguistic context. We may even prophesy, cast out demons, and perform miracles in His name and still hear the words, "I never knew you; depart from Me ..."[21]

Seek Him.

Renew your mind and be transformed in that renewal as you clothe yourself in the good and acceptable, and perfect will of God.[22] He is unchanging and unfathomable, but His mercies are new every morning. He is good to you. He is your portion.[23] He will grant you the spirit of wisdom and revelation so you can know Him more.[24]

The more you know Him, the more you will be overwhelmed by His great love for you. You will become filled with joy, and your heart will be at rest. You will be at peace no matter what is happening in your life.

Stand before Him and gaze deeply into His eyes as you declare, "I do." Meet with Him every day and determine to explore the heights, depth, and breadth of His love for you. The personality of the Trinity is complex and delightful and will take all of eternity to explore to the fullest. But begin today. Fix your eyes on Jesus and trust that knowing Him is the most wonderful thing imaginable.

I really enjoy having breakfast with Jesus. Every time I walk into the café, my expectations are high. I expect to meet with Father, or have a conversation with Jesus, or sit and see things through Holy Spirit's eyes. They speak to me. It is regular time I have set aside that keeps my heart aflame. I rarely miss this opportunity.

It was a Friday morning, concluding a very busy week. I rolled over and looked at the clock. "It's so late," I mumbled as I swung my legs over the edge of the bed and rubbed my eyes. I was exhausted. Usually, I wake up early and refreshed, ready to start the day, but a lot was happening, and my body was just tired.

I picked up my phone and opened my calendar app. The day was jam-packed with things that needed to be done, and it was too late in the morning for my usual routine of extended quiet time with God over coffee, and I was disappointed I had overslept. "I really want to have breakfast with You," I whispered a prayer. I felt irritable— annoyed that I had overslept and just a little cranky from feeling fatigued.

"Sweetheart," Paul called out cheerfully, "why don't I take you to breakfast this morning?"

I don't really have time for that; I thought to myself as I looked at my to-do list for the day. I wanted to say no. *Paul knows how much my Central Market appointment with Holy Spirit means to me; he knows how late it is already and how much I need to get done today. He doesn't really even eat breakfast. Why is he asking me today?*

"I'm not sure," I called out. "I have a lot going on today. I don't think I have time."

Paul came in and kissed me on the forehead. "I insist," he said, "let's go grab something. You look like you could use a good breakfast to start the day."

I decided it was better to set aside my list and have breakfast with Paul, but it felt like an imposition on my time with God. I got dressed and tried to reset my mind. Paul and I rarely ever had breakfast together. He doesn't ever eat a big breakfast. Paul is frugal enough that he doesn't like paying for something so easily prepared at home.

So, for a man who doesn't care a thing about breakfast and doesn't even really drink "fancy" coffees being so resolute to take me out that morning, I didn't want to spoil it by being grumpy.

We went to the Starbucks down the road from our home, and as we sat and chatted, I found I was there but not fully present. Then it dawned on me how special it was that he had taken time out to do something he knew I loved, even though it was not his thing. I pulled myself into the moment, and as I looked into Paul's eyes, and began to thank God for him.

Now, I must tell you that I have long worked on having conversations with a person while being attuned to and engaged with the Trinity. I can't really even tell you how I do this, but after such deep communion with Them, they are present in my spirit as I speak out loud to the person I am conversing with. So, as I looked into Paul's eyes and listened to the sound of his voice, my spirit began to say, "Thank You, Daddy, for Paul." But Holy Spirit replaced "Paul" with "Your Son, Jesus." My heart whispered, "Thank You, Daddy, for Your Son, Jesus," and I was moved to tears.

I hugged Paul affectionately as we parted ways for the day, but all morning I was moved by what happened at breakfast. "You wanted to have breakfast with Jesus, right?" Father said to me.

"Yes," I answered, "yes, I really did."

"Spending time with Paul—who is in Christ *(using Apostle Paul's terms)* is spending time with Jesus," God pointed out.

"You're right!" I marveled. I have often heard it being said that when God wants to give you a gift, He wraps it in a person, and I wondered how many times I missed the gift He gave me because I didn't know how to receive the person He put in my path. This morning, I wanted to have breakfast with Jesus. I was tired. Fatigued in my body. Weary from so many tasks pulling me in different directions, and I thought how nice it would be to actually sit across from Jesus and speak to Him in flesh and blood.

He did that for me. He showed up in Paul. Paul showed up to me as Christ and lavished his affection and attention and care upon me. He conversed with me, and the things—even the minor details—of my life were important to him. The Jesus in Paul ministered to me that morning. Like the Shulamite woman in the Song of Solomon, I was lovesick—waiting and looking for my Bridegroom. And He showed up to meet me.

God's answers to my prayers are creative and not just outside of the box, but as if the box does not exist—there is no box at all. He can answer me any way He pleases. I have learned I cannot dictate the terms of His answer or predetermine what He will do, when He will do it, or how He will do it. He loves me and seems to enjoy surprising me and demonstrating His affection for me in unexpected ways.

God loves me and seems to enjoy surprising me and demonstrating His affection for me in unexpected ways.

Have you ever met a bride who refused gifts? Have you ever encountered a bride who did not want her name assigned to what was rightfully hers upon marrying the groom?

Me either.

I spent twenty-six years in banking. When people get married and their last name changes, the couple comes in and makes all their accounts joint accounts. They become each other's beneficiaries—100% of life insurance, checking, savings, investment, and retirement accounts become joint property. If there is a trust, then the spouse is added as a trustee. From that moment, the husband owns everything the wife has, and the wife owns everything the husband has. (Unless there is a prenuptial agreement—but in Christ, there are no pre-nups! Divorce is not an option!)

When you are part of a joint account, you have the authority to do everything. You can deposit and withdraw. You can direct funds and administrate assets.

Paul and I have been married for a long time. The longer we are married, the more we think alike. We are one flesh, and we are also one in the Spirit. Our priorities, our values, and our instincts align with each other. In our family, Paul is the head, and he has the final say. I am his valued helpmeet, and he listens to my counsel, hears my heart, and knows that I am supportive, intelligent, and experienced. My desires carry great weight with him. Still, I submit to his authority, and my heart trusts in him. My assets are his, and his are mine. We do things together. There isn't even a matter of getting permission; we just naturally discuss things and move forward in agreement.

When I became the bride of Christ, He put me as a joint heir on His account. Everything that is His became mine. It is not 50/50. I have access to all that He has, all that He is. It is 100/100. We are one.

Children may have a portion of an inheritance—a bride has access to the entire estate.

Children may have a portion of an inheritance—a bride has access to the entire estate.

No longer that outsider with an orphan spirit, striving just to belong. No longer just His servant—joyful and glad to be about His business, but with limited access and authority. Now, also, no longer just His child, I have become His bride.

As I learn how to administrate God's estate and function in Kingdom authority, I realize I have so much more to learn. What an adventure lies ahead! Every day with Jesus is sweeter than the day before. Every moment in His presence opens up realms of possibilities and opportunities to function as He has created me and to bring Him pleasure and joy as I delight myself in Him.

Like the beautiful bride in Armenia who danced with abandon before her groom, that is how I want to approach Jesus. I am my Beloved's, and He is mine—I only have eyes for Him!

ENDNOTES

1. Song of Songs 2:14, TPT.
2. Revelation 19:7-9, NIV.
3. Isaiah 54:5, NKJV.
4. Samuel 25:39b-42, NLT.
5. Quote attributed to Jen Wilkin, Bible teacher.
6. See Matthew 10:30 and Luke 12:7.
7. See Psalm 139:14.
8. Ephesians 2:10, TPT.
9. See 1 Peter 2:9.
10. See Isaiah 61:1, Luke 4:18, and 1 John 2:20, 2:27.
11. Ezekiel 16:4-14, NLT.
12. See Ephesians 5:25-29.
13. See 2 Corinthians 5:7.
14. See Galatians 5:16.
15. See Micah 6:8.
16. See Deuteronomy 5:33.
17. Zechariah 3:7, ESV.
18. Romans 12:1-2, MSG.
19. Job 22:28, KJV.
20. Psalm 19:14, TPT.
21. See Matthew 7:21-23, NKJV.
22. See Romans 12:2.
23. See Lamentations 3:22-24.
24. See Ephesians 1:17.

Chapter Eight

INVITATION

*God conceals the revelation of His Word
in the hiding place of His glory.*

*But the honor of kings is revealed by how
thoroughly they search out the deeper
meaning of all that God says.*[1]

SOLOMON

Paul spoke of mysteries—things we cannot know unless God reveals them to us by His Spirit, no matter how hard we may try to figure them out on our own. This is a blessing. If we could know God by our own reasoning or imagination, we would create Him in our image—as we think or want Him to be in our minds rather than as He is. The limitation of our minds would limit Him.

God could never be that small.

That faith is both a mystery and an adventure is by God's design. Faith is meant to be an ongoing journey of discovery and exploration. God reveals Himself to us as we are ready to receive His revelation.

God reveals Himself to us as we are ready to receive His revelation. How wonderful that our intellect and abilities are removed from the equation regarding our relationship with God— the Triune Being, the Divine Mystery. It is exhilarating. It is He who sparks the desire in our hearts for Him, and the moment we respond, He lovingly breathes on our embers until they burst into radiant flames, illuminating His nature and character. Our curiosity and obedience bring kindling wood to the fire; our worship and our praise pour the oil that keeps it burning hot.

The more we know God, the more we desire to know God. The more we desire to know God, the more of Him we know. It is a beautiful cycle that takes us into the depths and breadths of His love for us and our fulfillment in Him.

Our flawed, broken human relationships sometimes hinder our ability to experience God as He is rather than God as we think Him to be. Because we have learned how to relate to God by how we have related to others, when those earthly relationships are dysfunctional, or worse, abusive, it can lead us to put up walls of protection around our hearts—even from the very One who could mend them.

I shared my story with you because as I reflected on how God loved me through the progression of my walk with Him, He began to reveal the mystery of the journey to me. My story is unique to my experience—growing up in India as a good Catholic girl, immigrating to Canada, then the United States, becoming financially secure, resisting the role of "pastor's wife," having a crisis of identity, then the loving invitation of the Father, and becoming who I am today. But my story is also familiar—feeling like an outsider; practicing a religion without life; making your own way as you self-provide, self-comfort, and self-motivate; longing for something meaningful—something more. You probably found yourself inside these pages.

I shared my journey through these stages: outsider, insider, servant, friend, daughter, and bride with purpose. My progression through these realities may not be all that uncommon. But too many I encounter are stuck as servants or as friends, perhaps even coming to experience Him as His child but never venturing into the intimate communion as His bride. It is my hope that you will open your heart to know Him as all these things, and that you will be hungry to experience more of Him—more of Them (Father, Son, and Holy Spirit).

God must guide you. You cannot force your way into understanding. He must reveal Himself to you as your Savior, your King, your Friend, your Father, and your Bridegroom. But there is a wonderful exchange that takes place when our hearts become hungry.

He satisfies.

As we end our time together, I have put together a brief review of each relationship stage with God. See what resonates with you and determine where your relationship with God is right now so you can grow hungry to know Him more—to seek out the mystery and receive the revelation He has for you and go with Him *Beyond the Veil.*

OUTSIDER

Awake, you who sleep,
Arise from the dead,
and Christ will give you light.[2]

THE BRIDEGROOM KING

When you are an outsider, you feel like you don't fit in, like you don't quite belong. As an outsider, you believe that others receive better things than you. You feel that there is something you must do so you can belong—perform, achieve. You become fiercely independent because interdependence is too risky. Relying on others has let you down, so things are up to you. This can manifest as an orphan spirit where you take on the responsibility of providing for yourself, motivating yourself, and comforting yourself. Your trust is very low, and you rely on your own abilities. Even so, you long to belong. You are tired of being a misfit with your nose pressed against the glass while others are inside, where it is warm and joyful, and full of life.

INSIDER

———— ·ᘓ·ᘏ·ᘓ· ————

Arise, my dearest.
Hurry, my darling.
Come away with me!
I have come as you have asked to draw
you to my heart and lead you out.
For now is the time, my beautiful one.[3]

THE BRIDEGROOM KING

As an insider, you experience Jesus as your Savior. When you receive Christ into your heart, your soul reaches for God in hunger, and you begin to open your heart to the things of the Spirit. As an insider, you go from being spiritually dead to becoming alive. You are an infant, not yet understanding how the Kingdom works, but you are alive! You can come in from the cold and warm your soul in the presence of Love. At last, you begin to find community, and you begin to believe that you *could* belong. Your identity is awakened, and hope kindles.

SERVANT

*The season has changed,
the bondage of your barren winter has ended,
and the season of hiding is over and gone.
The rains have soaked the earth.*[4]

THE BRIDEGROOM KING

As a servant, you experience God as your King. As your heart of stone is exchanged for a heart of flesh, you learn how to surrender yourself to your sovereign Lord willingly. In time, you learn to serve Him without thought of profit or reward but because God is your great King. You do it in faithfulness and obedience, with humility and joy. You move from the foyer and gain access to the interior rooms of the Kingdom. As a servant, you do not yet feel you can have a seat at the table, but you are now qualified to help prepare them for others. Your relationship with God is largely viewed as cause and effect. If you obey, you receive blessings. So God's faithfulness to you may be seen as a result of your actions. As a servant, it is easy to be stuck in performance and achievement as the price of belonging. There may even be a latent fear or concern that you could still be dismissed if you aren't good enough.

But as a servant in the King's house, you learn His preferences—His likes and dislikes—and what delights Him. You start picking up the language and customs of the Kingdom. As you obey His requests, you eventually start anticipating them, and as you begin to serve with a glad heart, you no longer need to be told what to do. It comes naturally. You grow bolder in your approach of the King, and you bring Him your list of requests and petition Him.

FRIEND

... and left it bright with blossoming flowers.
The season for singing and pruning
the vines has arrived.
I hear the cooing of doves in our
land, filling the air with songs to
awaken you and guide you forth.[5]

THE BRIDEGROOM KING

What a joy when you at last experience God as your friend! Your time as a servant has taught you He is worthy of a deeper level of trust. Now as His friend, you have intimate exchanges of thought and experience. You can be vulnerable and risk being fully known because you know, without a doubt, you are fully loved. You no longer question His acceptance of you. You know He loves you no matter what, and you begin to understand that His blessings are based on His goodness, not yours.

As His friend, you find that you desire to embrace all He has for you, even if you do not understand it or know how to appropriate it. You no longer come to Him with lists and beg for His attention to your requests. You now approach Him for the joy of spending time together. Friends break bread together. Share life. Swap stories. Laugh. Cry. Sometimes just sit in silence for the pure joy of fellowship and not the purpose of industry.

God is with you in the good times and the difficult times in equal measure. He is a forever friend; you do not need to prove

God is a forever friend; you do not need to prove your love.

your love. You have no need to check off boxes to demonstrate discipline, devotion, or loyalty. You now know that your actions do not influence His affection.

Friends speak each other's language—in fact, they develop a language of their very own. You still serve Him, but now not as a discipline of your will but as a natural expression of your heart. Your nature yields to His as your mind is renewed.

Now you sit at the table. You have access to His family and His household. As God's friend, you begin to experience His personality, humor, affection, and playfulness. You grow more confident in sharing your secrets with Him, and your trust deepens. You talk to Him less formally and feel accepted like you have never before experienced.

DAUGHTER

Can you not discern this new day of
destiny breaking forth around you?
The early signs of purpose and
plans are bursting forth.
The budding vines of new life are
now blooming everywhere.
The fragrance of their flowers whispers,
"There is change in the air."
Arise, my love, my beautiful companion,
and run with me to a higher place.
For now is the time to arise
and come away with me.[6]

THE BRIDEGROOM KING

You come to relate to God as your Father. You realize that He chose you long before you ever chose Him. Not only do you sit at the table, but you freely enter and participate in the conversation instead of just being close enough to overhear what He is saying to others. You are God's child! You are born of the Spirit, an heir—a joint heir with Jesus!

Regardless of how your earthly parents were, you begin to know God as a good Father, one who sacrifices for His children. Provides for them. Educates, clothes, feeds, loves, and nurtures them. It is an unbreakable bond. You were made in His image—you look like Him! You bear His likeness, and He has given you the authority and responsibility to have dominion over the earth.

What a change takes place in you as you discover God as a loving, invested, caring Father. All remnants of an orphan spirit—where you had to pull your weight and earn your place—are dislodged. Achievement and performance are no longer the foundation of your experience.

Daughters think differently than servants or friends. They have the security, identity, and privilege of belonging to the family and being a member of the household, entitled to all the privileges of their birthright. Daughters can help themselves to the refrigerator without special permission. You learn that you are authorized to partake of all the blessings of the household. You belong—you have a permanent residence of abiding. As you entered the blessings of sonship, you began to experience God as your Father—as Daddy—and the Kingdom of heaven begins to open up before you.

> **Daughters have the security, identity, and privilege of belonging to the family.**

There are vast rooms to explore in His Kingdom, and as His daughter, you are allowed to go into every single one! You now have a deep level of trust and experience wave upon wave of love. You marvel at His goodness, His extravagance, and His great grace and mercy. You know you are His beloved child—His favorite!

BRIDE

*For you are my dove, hidden
in the split-open rock.
It was I who took you and hid you up
high in the secret stairway of the sky.
Let me see your radiant face
and hear your sweet voice.
How beautiful your eyes of worship
and lovely your voice in prayer.[7]*

THE BRIDEGROOM KING

At long last, you now experience Jesus as your Bridegroom King! God has been preparing you all along; you just need to cooperate with the process until you can be presented without spots, wrinkles, or blemishes. This is impossible on your own. There is no amount of performance or achievement, no level of discipline or obedience that can make you a spotless bride. It is Christ in you who presents you to the Father holy and without fault.

As His bride, your trust is so complete you totally surrender. You now bear His name and have access and authority to the joint accounts. You are His beneficiary and trustee. You own everything He has, and He owns all of you. A child has only a portion of the inheritance, but a bride can access the entire estate. As you grow in maturity and experience, He entrusts you with more and more. You begin administrating the estate and learning how to function in

As His bride, you own everything He has, and He owns all of you.

the Kingdom with the authority of Christ. Stretching before you is all the joy of your salvation, all the willing sacrifice of serving your King, all the delight of friendship with God, all the security, safety, and provision of trusting your Daddy, and now all the possibilities, opportunities, and adventures of walking beside the Bridegroom in beautiful intimacy and purity, clothed in beauty and lost in His love.

Will you come away with Him? Will you let Him draw you to His heart and lead you out? Will you leave your barrenness behind, allowing Him to drench your soul in the water of the Word and prune your vines until your heart is in full bloom?

A new day of destiny is breaking forth around you—new life in Him awaits. Run with Him to a higher place. Fix your gaze on His countenance and trust Him to reveal Himself to you daily. Life in the Spirit is more incredible than you can possibly imagine. Won't you say yes to His call?

The Bridegroom beckons you to go with Him *Beyond the Veil.*

ENDNOTES

1. Proverbs 25:2, TPT.
2. Ephesians 5:14, NKJV.
3. Song of Songs 2:10, TPT.
4. Song of Songs 2:11, TPT.
5. Song of Songs 2:12, TPT.
6. Song of Songs 2:13, TPT.
7. Song of Songs 2:14, TPT.

Meet the Author

Yvonne Allen could be described as a deep river. Her speech is never superficial because her thoughts are intentional, and her desires are eternal. She never gets distracted, distraught, or pulled off course because she is steadfast with the Lord. She consistently has a walk with the Holy Spirit that inspires others to know Him more. She communes with the Godhead and is truly led by the Spirit. As a result, Yvonne has a very happy marriage, children who fear the Lord in a healthy way, and she exhibits heaven on earth in her health, prosperity, and relationships. She exemplifies what it is to really be a Christian—not just talking about it, but demonstrating it through her lifestyle. She is a living epistle known and read of all men. If you have the privilege to know her, you will get to meet one facet of Jesus, as expressed through her personality and calling. Yvonne is a mature Christian, believing, talking, and conducting her life unwaveringly in a Christlike way. Clearly, she has been with Jesus.

With no natural head start in life, Yvonne Allen is a successful business owner. She grew up in India, giving it her very best before immigrating to Canada, and now makes her home in the United States, where she has grown and prospered in every way. Her success is a combination of God's favor, combined with obedience, hard work, and diligence.

Yvonne lives in Southlake, Texas, with her husband, Paul. Together they have two wonderful married children with families of their own. She is full of joy and always fun to be around.

To learn more or invite Yvonne to speak:
Y V O N N E A L L E N . C O M

Made in the USA
Middletown, DE
01 September 2023

37512150R00099